# ADMINISTRATIVE

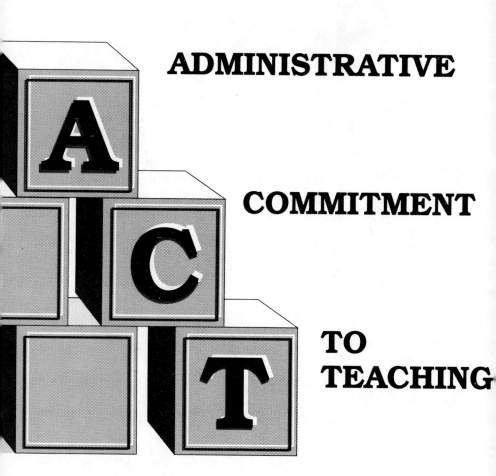

# COMMITMENT

# TO
# TEACHING

Leslie H. Cochran, Provost
Southeast Missouri State University

STEP UP, INC.
Cape Girardeau, Missouri

# ADMINISTRATIVE

## COMMITMENT

## TO

## TEACHING

Leslie H. Cochran, Provost,
Southeast Missouri State University

Copyright © 1989 by STEP UP, Inc.

STEP UP, Inc.
Publications Division
2 Spanish Street Court
Cape Girardeau, MO 63701

Library of Congress Catalog Card Number: 89-91743

Printed in the United States of America


**Library of Congress Cataloging in Publication Data**

Cochran, Leslie H., 1939-
  *Administrative Commitment to Teaching*
  Bibliography: p 177
  1.  College teaching - United States

  2.  Universities and colleges - United States - Teaching

  3.  Universities and colleges - United States - Administration

  I.  Title

# Administrative Commitment to Teaching

## Table of Contents

# PREFACE

Excellence in the classroom has long been valued as the most essential responsibility for college faculty members. Clearly, the teaching and learning processes are the essence of higher education. While the importance of teaching is unmistakable, there has been a long standing debate over the critical nature of teaching and the value given to teaching in higher education. More recently, substantive questions regarding the commitment to teaching have been raised from various sectors within and without the academic community. Concerns over quality and accountability have elevated this issue to a new pinnacle.

While the call for reform has produced volumes of rhetoric, much of the debate has been limited to glossed-over superlatives and generalities. In reality, the issue has been raised, but little has been done to change policies or address the traditional publish-or-perish syndrome. **Administrative Commitment to Teaching** is directed at this fundamental problem and provides tangible, research-based insights on how to make a stronger commitment to teaching. It segments the issue and presents hundreds of examples and illustrations on how improvements can be made. It recognizes, too, that change initiatives must be present on a number of fronts and must be started in a planned manner. Suggestions for change are woven into the concept that faculty members must routinely practice their art and stand ready to demonstrate their teaching and scholarly competence. The challenge for the future is to produce teaching scholars so instructional excellence can be placed at the apex of higher education.

A book of this magnitude could only be accomplished through the combined efforts of many friends and colleagues. Several individuals at Southeast Missouri State University directly contributed to the completion of this project. I would like to extend a special tribute to Dalton Curtis and Jim Eison. Both of these individuals made invaluable contributions in terms of ideas and suggestions. Their professional insights and editorial advice significantly contributed to the overall quality of the text. I greatly appreciate, too, the special efforts of Dorothy Allen and Sheila Caskey who spent hours previewing the manuscript and sharing their reactions. Also, Roy Farris deserves special recognition. He dedicated hours of personal time to improve the readability of the manuscript and refine the presentation of the concepts.

A special commendation must also be extended to Deborah Blumenberg for her many hours and sincere dedication to perfecting, preparing, and organizing the manuscript. Without her diligence and patience, the project could not have been completed. Steve Chatman made an extraordinary effort to develop and streamline the data collection, statistical treatment, and data analysis procedures. There are many other colleagues whose suggestions led to improvement in the survey instrument who deserve special comment. Likewise, I am indebted to the over 1300 chief academic officers whose participation in the original research made this work possible. Through the combined efforts of these individuals, I am hopeful that **Administrative Commitment to Teaching** will make a difference in the future of higher education.

L.H.C.

# Chapter One

## COLLEGE AND THE TEACHING PROFESSION

Teaching in college has long been a highly respected profession. Yet, college teaching has recently assumed a new importance in the higher education community. An increasing number of scholars have begun to give serious attention to the issue of quality in teaching. What was the norm a decade or two ago is no longer acceptable. An outstanding researcher cannot continue to be only a mediocre instructor. Nor can a fine classroom performer show no evidence of current scholarship. The demands placed on members of the professoriate require excellence in both teaching and scholarship. Faculty members and administrators alike must accept the challenge of eliminating the false dichotomy between teaching and scholarship so the concept of a teaching scholar can truly emerge. Scholarship must bolster teaching, and teaching must foster learning and further scholarship.

From its rudimentary beginnings in Bologna, Paris, and Oxford, the professoriate has been established as a dynamic evolving force in society. The accolades and contributions of higher education have been enumerated throughout history. In the United States, the academic community has been instrumental in the artistic, economic, literary, scientific, social, and technological advancement of our culture. Much of our international respect has evolved from the work of college professors and the contributions of approximately three thousand colleges and universities across the nation.

The roots of American higher education can be traced to the General Court of Massachusetts, which established Harvard in 1636, and to other early imitations of Oxford and Cambridge that emerged in the Colonial era. These efforts gave rise to the private liberal arts college that was to dominate higher education for the next two hundred years. Beginning in the last half of the nineteenth century, the framework for today's American academic profession started to emerge. Three major developments dramatically influenced the profession and shaped the destiny of those who now dedicate their lives to higher education. First, the fundamentally diverse nature of the American system was created and its growth accelerated at a staggering rate. As the number of institutions increased, diversity in higher education became more prevalent than similarity, and differing faculty interests gave rise to a plethora of disciplines. Second, a hierarchy of prestige produced by the formation of graduate schools started to shape the role of faculty members. Influenced by the German emphasis on research, leading scientists and scholars were primarily attracted to those institutions which set out to become great research universities. Third, spurred by the Morrill Acts of 1862 and 1890, the state university movement brought a new clientele and further diversification to the American scene. Faculty members were called upon to provide "something for everyone" on a relatively unselective basis. As a result of these forces, American higher education became a unique blend of undergraduate education, specialized research, graduate study, and professional education. For the professoriate, the changes were just as dramatic. Faculty members gained new roles and responsibilities, greater specialization, increased authority and power, and expanded control over the profession. Burton Clark (3:16) summarized it best in **The Academic Life** when he wrote that:

> What changed within the local hierarchies to give influence to faculty was their gathering control of knowledge brought about by research-driven specialization. Once the research ethic was in the driver's seat, there could no longer be a common curriculum taught by men of general learning whose responsibility in the first instance would be the moral character of the young. When the universities sought the rewards of research, they also moved toward a modern profession of academics in which self-government would be strengthened. They created settings in which professors would acquire primacy in determining the precise nature of their work -- what they would teach and what they would research -- and would have more than a passing influence, subject by subject and classroom by classroom, in determining who they served. The academic guild came late to American higher education, but come it did, and on the back of fragmenting bundles of

knowledge that allowed "teachers" to become "professors" by acquiring the authority of arcane knowledge.

The post World War II era brought, through the GI Bill, a new clientele to higher education and ushered in a series of new themes. Higher education's agenda changed dramatically from the post Sputnik attention to science and mathematics, to an effort to liberalize general education, to a focus on career education, and to the tenets of "basic education". During the last twenty-five years, a series of relatively new but interrelated themes has emerged in a fairly consistent pattern. While it is probably premature to suggest that the current interest in college teaching will emerge as the dominant influence to affect the profession, there are strong indications that college teaching will become one of higher education's most important agendas in the 1990's. Should the attention being given to this initiative continue to grow, the role of teaching has the potential of reshaping the internal value structure and very fabric of higher education. The opportunity to change dramatically the role of teaching has been elevated to an unmatched level. The profession is currently poised to reassess totally the importance of teaching and to suggest avenues that reunite the fundamental roles of teaching and scholarship. The current themes of faculty renewal, curricular reform, and professional accountability, along with changes in the employment conditions of faculty, suggest the emergence of a new framework for higher education.

---

*... there are strong indications that college teaching will become one of higher education's most important agendas in the 1990's ... the role of teaching has the potential of reshaping the internal value structure and very fabric of higher education.*

---

## Faculty Renewal

Faculty members throughout higher education have long been interested in improving their professional competence. Institutions have utilized numerous means to respond to these subject matter needs -- sabbatical leaves, faculty exchanges, conferences and workshops, postdoctoral study, etc. The student protests of the 1960s, however, produced a marked change in the level of professional attention to this area and increased the amount of concern for faculty renewal at the institutional level. Demands were heard for faculty to become more responsive to student needs, to provide more effective instruction, and to demonstrate a higher level of commitment to curricular improvement. There was a call to formalize the process of faculty renewal. In the 1970s instructional development units sprang up across the nation. High priority was given to course planning and evaluation, instructional materials development, and workshops to improve instruction of subject matter. (It is interesting to note, however, that these early efforts paid virtually no attention to the teaching/learning process and how course content could best be conveyed to the student.)

By the mid seventies, the faculty renewal movement gained a broader base of support. Student demands were converted to a new type of consumerism. Aroused state legislatures called for increased accountability. New educational techniques emerged and the use of alternative teaching styles fostered a new attitude among segments of the professoriate. Clear changes began to emerge in the profession that demanded a new level of teaching and scholarly competence for individuals pursuing a career in higher education. The evaluation of teaching became commonplace. The professional educator was influenced, too, by changes in the number and types of students. While these were contributing factors, the sudden interest in faculty development can be linked primarily to the tighter job market for professors and a dwindling level of financial support for higher education.

The last decade has witnessed a significant increase in the emphasis given to teaching. Institutionally sponsored workshops, seminars, and other programs have been implemented to help faculty members acquire knowledge, skill, sensitivity, and techniques of teaching. Programs that support competitive faculty grants and released time for instructional improvement have been established. Inservice courses and workshops to improve classroom performance have become increasingly popular. Feedback programs designed to assist individual faculty members to improve their instructional capacity are under way on many campuses. Programs designed to help the first-year faculty member have become more prevalent. Foundation support has been particularly effective in spawning many of these new initiatives. Likewise, several professional associations have initiated projects to assist their members to become more effective teachers.

# Curricular Reform

The curricular reform movement, particularly at the undergraduate level, has emerged as one of the foremost characteristics of the 1980's. Efforts to rehabilitate the undergraduate curriculum are underway in virtually every segment of the academic community. There is a new surge of interest in general education with over two-thirds of institutions reporting that major reviews of their programs are moving forward (6). Over eighty percent of all campuses are now reexamining their degree requirements. Institutions are struggling to give proper meaning and definition to a degree, a major, a minor, etc. Similarly, specialized programs are under pressure from national commissions and accrediting bodies to bring about substantive changes. Within this context, reformers have attempted to give higher status to teaching and to revise tenure and promotion policies to reflect these changes.

The most far reaching and encompassing report that addressed the full breadth of these issues was **Integrity in the College Curriculum**. This 1985 publication from the Association of American Colleges pointedly characterized the disarray of the bachelor's degree; portrayed the nature of academe's curricular paralysis; delineated the shortcomings of requirements for degrees, liberal arts, and majors; and attacked the professoriate for its unwillingness to face its obligation for college teaching. A second influential publication was the 1987 book by Ernest L. Boyer entitled **College: The Undergraduate Experience in America**. This in-depth analysis of baccalaureate education argued for substantive curricular reform of the entire undergraduate experience. Again, restrictions caused by curricular fragmentation and specialization were cited; divided faculty loyalties among scholarship, research, and teaching were discussed; and internal and external tensions affecting the academic community were analyzed.

Fundamental to the reform movement are the actual changes occurring on campuses throughout the nation. While general education reform is the most notable, other forces are also at work that bring attention to the need to improve teaching. For example, cross-disciplinary efforts to internationalize the curriculum and to incorporate writing-across-the-curriculum place teaching within a broader context. Calls for instructional approaches that promote active learning suggest a need for re-orientation of the entire teaching and learning process. Also, freshman experience courses introduce a new level of faculty involvement into the educational continuum.

# Professional Accountability

One of the remarkable anomalies in American higher education has been the absence of internal and external measures of institutional and social accountability. Some sectors of the profession are insulted whenever questions are raised about the quality of programs, the effectiveness of instruction, or the productivity of faculty members. While part of the larger reform movement, the question of accountability looms so large on the college teaching agenda that it deserves special attention. There is widespread skepticism about the quality of higher education. There is a public sense that academic standards are too low. There are demands from state legislatures to measure student learning outcomes. There are ongoing debates within the professoriate regarding program review, outcomes assessment, and the evaluation of teaching.

The issue of quality is grounded in the conviction that evaluation ought to be an integral component of the structure that undergirds higher education. Critics emphasize that institutional goals, program objectives, course content, and the manner in which instruction is provided must stand the test. Institutions must be able to demonstrate that they have indeed provided the knowledge, skills, and understanding they have professed to provide. Clearly, there is a need to develop and refine evaluative procedures. These demands for change are substantial and extend far beyond what might be seen as simple refinement; they have placed the profession in a defensive position. The professoriate must respond positively to reassert the importance of teaching and scholarship. It must seize the current opportunity to demonstrate the inherent quality of the academy.

---

*Clearly, there is a need to develop and refine evaluative procedures. These demands for change are substantial and extend far beyond what might be seen as simple refinement; they have placed the profession in a defensive position.*

---

The evaluation of instruction is an integral component of the accountability question. The recent work of Peter Seldin has demonstrated that interest in evaluating teaching is on the upswing; that the quality of evaluative instruments has vastly improved; and that procedures can be put in place to effectively evaluate instruction. Effective accountability measures cannot be achieved without the systematic assessment of instruction. If teaching is to assume its rightful role on the college campus, the evaluation of instruction must include the full range of a faculty member's responsibility. Attention must be directed to the level of professional competence as measured in terms of content expertise, classroom preparation, organization of instructional material, and the actual classroom presentation. As institutions move in this direction, faculty resistance will mount and administrative mistakes will be made. While there is no perfect system, the goal must be to make teaching a higher priority for colleges and universities across the nation. This goal can be accomplished only by producing varied and reliable means that demonstrate the overall effectiveness of what transpires in the classroom and what occurs as a result of instruction.

## Employment Conditions

The current and projected employment conditions for faculty members present a set of contradictions. As a group, faculty members are committed to the teaching enterprise, they are dedicated to their disciplines, and they strongly identify with a common academic culture. While they espouse these values, their individual attitudes vary considerably. Many are concerned about a deteriorating work environment characterized by decreasing economic leverage, dwindling mobility, and weakening morale. Others see a series of conflicting signals about the priorities of scholarship, rewards, instruction, collegiality, and advising. Still others question the various changes (assessment, curriculum, evaluation, etc.) that produce uneasy tensions.

These issues are not new and are not likely to change dramatically over the next decade or two. There are, however, emerging employment patterns that will intensify the attention given to the basic teaching functions. These new conditions will increase the expectations of faculty members, present new personal and institutional opportunities, require additional institutional support, and promote an expanded need for an evaluative data base by which individuals can demonstrate their teaching effectiveness.

Five pieces of the puzzle of the future are already in place. First, the "graying" of the faculty is moving steadily forward with projections that by the year 2000 over fifty percent of the faculty will be over 55 years of age. These changes will likely produce greater maturity and stability, but increased support for faculty renewal and teaching enhancement activities will also need to be forthcoming. Second, the swift movement away from across-the-board pay increases to merit-based approaches will intensify demands upon faculty members to produce stronger measures and evidence of teaching effectiveness and instructional quality. Third, the academy will enjoy an expanded opportunity to hire new faculty members because of modest enrollment growth over the next decade. Significant changes will occur in the professoriate as a result of large proportions of faculty retirements. The 1960s employment bulge will produce critical shortages in most areas. Fourth, external demands for greater accountability will continue to affect the academy. Graduate Ph.D. programs, for example, will come under great pressure to add a teaching component to the program of those entering the college teaching profession. Fifth, and potentially the most volatile, is the planned elimination of the federally mandated 70 years of age retirement in the early 1990s. Regardless of the employment alternatives that evolve, demands for even greater teaching effectiveness evidence will likely increase. When these new conditions are combined with the ongoing trends to focus more attention on teaching and to evaluate teaching more systematically, it is clear that college teaching will assume a new identity in the years ahead.

## Future Agenda

While the momentum to place greater emphasis on college teaching has been on the upswing, the last five years has witnessed a dramatic explosion of reports, conferences, and publications on the topic. The recent surge of interest in teaching is a natural extension of the public calls for reform of the public schools which occurred during the early part of the eighties. In 1983 alone, five major publications focused on this issue -- **A Nation at Risk** by the National Commission on Excellence in Education; **A Place Called School** by John Goodlad; **Educating Americans for the 21st Century** by the National Science Foundation; **High School: A Report on Secondary Education in America** by Ernest Boyer; and **Schools and College: Partnerships in Education** by Gene Maeroff.

This trend spread to the collegiate level with the National Institute of Education's release in 1984 of **Involvement in Learning: Realizing the Potential of American Higher Education**. The Association of American College's **Integrity in the College**

**Curriculum** (1985) and **A New Vitality in General Education** (1988) provided specific directions for the future. **To Secure the Blessings of Liberty** (1986) from the American Association of State Colleges and Universities added recommendations for sweeping changes. Finally, Boyer's book on **College: The Undergraduate Experience in America** provided the essential data base and analysis to suggest a new vision for higher education in the future.

College teaching has become a centerpiece of the agenda for much of the higher education community. The recent conferences of the American Association for Higher Education have dealt specifically with teaching. Professional associations in many disciplines have added sessions on teaching to their conference format. **The Teaching Professor** newsletter, with articles on improving teaching on campus, has gained instant attention from a large segment of the profession. Numerous articles by Patricia Cross, Wilbert McKeachie, and Peter Seldin have provided concrete examples and strategies on how to improve college instruction and its evaluation. Several national studies are underway at the University of Michigan's National Center for Research to Improve Postsecondary Teaching and Learning to address some of the commonly held perceptions and myths regarding the role of teaching on campus.

The needs of the higher education community are many, but the commitment to teaching must start at the top. In October 1987, thirty-seven presidents and chancellors representing all sectors of the academic community accepted this challenge and met to pledge their support. In an open letter (19) to their colleagues across the nation, they called for a concerted effort to reaffirm the importance of teaching and to raise its standing within the profession.

> On our own campuses, a debate has emerged about how prospective teachers should be prepared. We sense in these and other developments an unprecedented opportunity to transform the nature of teaching and the teaching profession ... First we can make a personal commitment to speak out for education and the importance of teaching at all levels. The problems of elementary and higher education are deeply intertwined. We must therefore become champions for the whole educational enterprise. To do this **credibly** is no easy task. It will require us to become more informed about the needs of our schools

and communities. It will further require us to address our own shortcomings. Only if we are seriously committed to the improvement of teaching in our own houses can we speak convincingly about the importance of high quality teaching in the schools ... Teaching is the first business of our universities, just as it is the first business of the primary and secondary schools across the country. Recognition of that deep community of profession should therefore underlie all our efforts.

The message for higher education is clear. The decade of the nineties presents an important opportunity to make college teaching the foremost priority of the profession. This transformation will not happen overnight, nor will the changes occur easily. It requires a willingness to debate the issues, to understand current research and evaluative strategies, and to construct procedures and policies to implement the new emphasis. Most of all, it requires an administrative commitment to teaching. Teaching is the preferred activity of over two-thirds of the faculty members across the nation, but it is not what is most frequently rewarded. The profession gives tremendous support to the value of teaching, but the value of teaching is often deflated. This mismatch between myth and reality must be addressed.

---

*The profession gives tremendous support to the value of teaching, but the value of teaching is often deflated. This mismatch between myth and reality must be addressed.*

---

# Chapter Two

## TEACHING ON CAMPUS

American higher education stands at the apex of the world's academic community. Its provision for universal student access is the envy of the world. It provides opportunity to all and unlimited choices of study to all. The more than two thousand baccalaureate-granting institutions provide a diverse array of educational experiences. The professors that toil in the academic halls are among the world's best and have produced notable scholarship in virtually all disciplines. Student accomplishments are, likewise, most remarkable. These successes are a tribute to those individuals who have dedicated their lives to the profession. What often seems to go unnoticed is the basic function that has contributed the most to these successes. Teaching is one of the fundamental processes that has distinguished the American system of higher education.

As sophisticated as higher education is in the United States, it has internal problems and its critics are many. Depending upon one's view, higher education has been criticized from virtually every possible perspective. The practice of teaching, however, is an interesting set of contradictions. The essential work of teaching maintains the system. It provides an unsurpassed avenue for intellectual discourse and debate. Teaching serves as a great source of intrinsic satisfaction and produces intense commitment from many academics. While prestige often comes from scholarly research and publications, most faculty members prefer teaching. Yet, the tension between teaching and research has never been fully resolved. The gap between duty and reward for teaching is commonly cited as a major dilemma for the academic community. Institutional leaders are often criticized for their seeming lack of interest in teaching. Further, the professoriate has been beleaguered by the controversy surrounding the evaluation of instruction.

*Teaching serves as a great source of intrinsic satisfaction and produces intense commitment from many academics. While prestige often comes from scholarly research and publications, most faculty members prefer teaching. Yet, the tension between teaching and research has never been fully resolved.*

## Perspectives of Teaching

The views toward teaching on the campuses across the nation vary so greatly that it is virtually impossible to state with clarity the exact nature of the basic teaching function. Diversity of attitudes can be seen among individuals and between specific types of institutions. Likewise, perceptions shift dramatically among students, faculties, and administrators. While perspectives may differ, it is important that base line data concerning faculty interests and work load commitments be presented. An assessment of faculty interest and use of their time suggests that a high level of time and energy is given to the teaching function. Three comparisons are particularly noteworthy.

First, Burton Clark (3), reporting on a 1984 survey of 2,896 faculty members by The Carnegie Foundation for the Advancement of Teaching, found that 70 percent of all faculty members had strong interests in teaching. Table 1 presents an array of the percentages of the faculty in various types of institutions responding to the question, "Do your interests lie primarily in teaching or in research?" The data indicate that in "research" universities, 35-45 percent of the faculty have strong teaching interests; in doctoral degree-granting universities, the numbers increase to roughly 55-75 percent; in comprehensive institutions strong teaching interests are at the 75 percent level; and in liberal arts colleges, they range from approximately 75 percent to 90 percent. It might also be noted that only 15 percent of faculty members at the research institutions report being heavily committed to research. The level of commitment to research is dramatically less at other types of institutions. Clearly, the professoriate has a high level of interest in the basic teaching function.

Second, as reported in an analysis of how faculty members spend their time, the same Carnegie Study indicates that teaching activities (direct and indirect) consume about 70 percent of the faculty's

## Table 1
## Percentage of Faculty
## Primary Interest in Teaching or Research
## By Type of Institution (3:86)

Question: "Do your interests lie primarily in teaching or in research? ... (1) Very heavily in research (2) In both, but leaning toward research (3) In both, but leaning toward teaching (4) Very heavily in teaching.

| Type of Institution | (1) Heavily in Research | (2) Both: Toward Research | (3) Both: Toward Teaching | (4) Heavily in Teaching |
|---|---|---|---|---|
| Research Universities I | 16 | 49 | 23 | 12 |
| Research Universities II | 15 | 40 | 27 | 18 |
| Doctoral-Granting Universities I | 8 | 34 | 36 | 22 |
| Doctoral-Granting Universities II | 6 | 18 | 45 | 31 |
| Comprehensive Universities and Colleges I | 3 | 22 | 34 | 41 |
| Comprehensive Universities and Colleges II | 3 | 22 | 35 | 40 |
| Liberal Arts Colleges I | 4 | 22 | 44 | 30 |
| Liberal Arts Colleges II | 1 | 9 | 27 | 63 |
| Two-Year Colleges and Institutions | 1 | 7 | 23 | 69 |
| All Institutions | 6 | 24 | 30 | 40 |

Permission: The Carnegie Foundation for the Advancement of Teaching.

time (see Table 2). While this proportion is substantial, other studies suggest that the 70 percent figure may be low when full consideration is given to student evaluation activities, lesson preparation, and other responsibilities intertwined in the teaching/learning process. Even when the comparison between direct instructional activities and research activities is made from these data, the teaching function dominates by more than a two-to-one ratio.

A third analysis of the data presented by Ernest Boyer (6) suggests that these proportions may be somewhat skewed, because 14 percent of the sample report devoting no time to classroom instruction. While the data reported in Table 3 are limited to

## Table 2
## Allocation of Faculty Work Hours at Four-Year
## Institutions By Median Hours Per Task (2:33)

|  | Hours | Percent |
|---|---|---|
| Direct Instructional Activities |  | 43.1 |
| Classroom Preparation | 6.9 |  |
| Undergraduate Instruction | 7.5 |  |
| Graduate Instruction | 1.3 |  |
|  | 15.7 |  |
|  |  |  |
| Indirect Instructional Activities |  | 26.4 |
| Advising | 3.0 |  |
| Office Hours | 5.3 |  |
| Counseling | 1.3 |  |
|  | 9.6 |  |
|  |  |  |
| Research Activities | 6.7 | 18.5 |
|  |  |  |
| Administrative Activities | 4.4 | 12.0 |
|  | 36.4 | 100 |

Permission: The Carnegie Foundation for the Advancement of Teaching

undergraduate instruction, the 26 percent figure for research institutions suggests that some individuals with full-time research
duties are likely to be included in the sample. Regardless of the
interpretation, the data clearly indicate that in terms of faculty
interests and allocation of their time, teaching is a high priority for
the vast majority of the professoriate.

## Table 3
## Average Number of Hours per Week Faculty Devote to
## Classroom Instruction in Undergraduate Courses
## (percentage responding) (6:21)

| Type of Institution | None | 1-4 | 5-10 | 11-20 | 20+ |
|---|---|---|---|---|---|
| All Institutions | 14 | 21 | 38 | 25 | 2 |
| Research Universities | 26 | 35 | 30 | 8 | 1 |
| Doctoral-Granting Universities | 14 | 24 | 41 | 19 | 2 |
| Comprehensive Universities/Colleges | 8 | 13 | 41 | 36 | 2 |
| Liberal Arts Colleges | 3 | 13 | 43 | 38 | 3 |

Permission: The Carnegie Foundation for the Advancement of Teaching

Quality teaching must be a primary concern of every faculty member who has instructional responsibilities. While some faculty members need to be pushed toward the exploration of authentic research, all institutions must encourage, support, and reward outstanding teaching. Boyer (6:126) vividly emphasized this point as he called for equal treatment for the teaching and research criteria at "research" institutions.

> At the same time research institutions also must aggressively support good teaching. After all, at large universities, where much of the research is conducted, two thirds or more of all students are undergraduates, and the push to publish, without an equal concern for teaching, can have a chilling effect on the classroom and be shockingly detrimental to the students.

> We conclude then that, at every research university, teaching should be valued as highly as research, and good teaching should be an equally important criterion for tenure and promotion. To expect faculty to be good researchers and good teachers is a demanding standard. Still, it is at the research university where the two come together, and faculty, at such institutions, should contribute effectively to both.

## Values Conflict

While teaching is the most fundamental activity on all college campuses, it has often been characterized as representing a mismatch between myth and reality. The teaching/learning process is the essence of what an institution of higher learning is all about, but somehow the manner in which these activities are practiced, nurtured, and rewarded leaves much to be desired. One could place blame for this disparity on various segments of the academic community or on particular social forces, but such attributions seem to miss the point. The contradictions could be ignored, but that, too, leaves little hope for change. These tensions require attention. To address each issue would require volumes, which is not the purpose at hand. Rather, some of the major conflicts are illustrated here to provide a more realistic context for the agenda ahead.

The preceding section regarding the perspectives of teaching identified a fundamental conflict present in the role of faculty. Faculty members at most institutions devote the vast majority of their time to the instructional process, and yet, these efforts are not fully rewarded. Providing appropriate rewards is often identified by faculty members as the first step toward establishing a balanced perspective between the importance of teaching and research. While faculty members cite the need for immediate changes in existing reward structures, other modifications will need to occur before significant adjustments are made in terms of rewards. Initiatives will need to be set in motion that create new instructional effectiveness data bases, establish expanded evaluation procedures, and facilitate in-class peer and administrative review of teaching activities. Existing levels of interest in these areas will not support the rewards needed to elevate teaching to the apex of academic values. Attitudes and actions that reinforce these changes need to become commonplace before all of the reward structures needed can be fully implemented. Isolated examples of what is possible already take the form of Outstanding Teaching Awards, Meritorious Teaching Recognition Programs, and Distinguished Teaching Professorships. Of course, the real battle to fully integrate the expanded perspectives on teaching effectiveness is centered in the mainstream areas of the faculty employment process -- selection and hiring, promotion, merit, tenure, and last, but certainly not least, faculty salaries. A more realistic view of such reform efforts suggests that reward systems will gradually be modified as new faculty evaluation procedures are introduced.

---

*Providing appropriate rewards is often identified by faculty members as the first step toward establishing a balanced perspective between the importance of teaching and research. While faculty members cite the need for immediate changes in existing reward structures, other modifications will need to occur before significant adjustments are made in terms of rewards.*

---

Annually, major research universities send away bright young teachers because of inadequacies in their records of research and scholarly activity. Administrators are regularly criticized for paying lip service to teaching excellence and then promoting individuals because of distinctive research records and prolific publication lists.

While the merits of individual cases may vary, the common perception is that research productivity regularly wins out over teaching. What has happened in most situations is that the institution has not clearly articulated its own values. Typically, when a new faculty member is terminated for lack of scholarly activity, the system has failed. Such faculty members have not been properly guided by their colleagues. The role of scholarship has not been effectively communicated. The new member has not properly assumed his/her professional responsibilities. Administrators have not demonstrated the distinction between the classroom performance on a short-term basis and the need to demonstrate professional disciplinary competence over an extended career. The system has similarly failed when the weak classroom instructor with a strong scholarly record is tenured or promoted. Again, deficiencies can be noted for all parties, and at all levels, but the major flaw rests with the departmental members who fail to evaluate their colleagues' teaching qualifications.

The evaluation of teaching, too, represents a series of value conflicts. Many in the professoriate demonstrate an inward fear of evaluation. Some faculty lack understanding of proper evaluative techniques and most mistrust colleague or administrative use of evaluative data. Clearly, a large segment of the profession narrowly limits the evaluation of instruction to the confines of the classroom. Each of these concerns represents an area of needed improvement within the academic community. Further, there is a need for the dissemination of better information about evaluating instruction. Instruments and data systems need to be improved, and the concepts underlying the evaluation of instruction need to be understood by all segments of the profession.

*Some faculty lack understanding of proper evaluative techniques and most mistrust colleague or administrative use of evaluative data. Clearly, a large segment of the profession narrowly limits the evaluation of instruction to the confines of the classroom.*

While each of these areas deserves attention, the narrow perspectives on the evaluation of instruction require specific attention. Current literature suggests that teaching can be evaluated effectively. While it is true that a substantial portion of the professoriate is neither interested in nor willing to undertake this task, if teaching is to be elevated, and if appropriate rewards are to be forthcoming, an evaluative base must be present. Data, insights, and input on teaching must be evidenced from a variety of sources. Most importantly, the evaluation of instruction must encompass the entire range of teaching activity. Faculty members must be conceived as teaching scholars. They must demonstrate disciplinary competence and, at the same time, reveal competence in the classroom. The evaluation of these basic ingredients must draw evidence that demonstrates teaching excellence in subject matter competence, content organizational competence, and classroom performance competence.

For most new faculty members entering the profession, the integral nature of teaching and scholarship is far more acceptable. While most may not embrace this duality with enthusiasm, they are more receptive to the concept and see the long-term benefits. These issues, however, present a major dilemma for a sizeable portion of the existing professoriate. Almost automatically, when an action is taken contrary to the perspective of the more senior faculty members, the cries of outrage are heard. "The rules have changed!" "How can I compete with these new faculty members?" "It's not fair!" "When I was hired, it was good enough to be an outstanding teacher!" The list goes on and in a sense many of these statements represent partial truth. In other cases, however, these perceptions can more likely be coupled with long-standing misunderstandings. Many faculty members have conveniently forgotten the importance of scholarship and practicing their own art.

Regardless of the reason, the profession must willingly acknowledge these differences and take steps to correct the situation. Higher education cannot be a static operation. The demands being placed on higher education are different today and the needs of society have become more diverse. The decades ahead will place even greater expectations on its professionals. (It is ironic to note that many academics who have accepted the professional challenge to pursue the unknown, to discover new knowledge, and to stimulate change within their own disciplines have such great difficulty in accepting these tenets for themselves and their own teaching.) Difficult as it may be, these demands must be addressed, and the governance structures of higher education must respond. Steps must be taken and support mechanisms introduced that move faculty members toward the goal of reaching their highest potential. The scholarship expectations of a professor with twenty years of experience need not be the same as those for the new assistant professor. On the other extreme, it is unacceptable to embrace the notion that institutions must simply wait until certain faculty members retire. The challenge rests with members of the academic community to concentrate on their disciplines and the students they serve. Both deserve more than has been given in the past, thereby resulting in better teaching and more scholarship.

The unrealistic separation of teaching and scholarship and the duality of a reward system that pits one against the other do not present a workable framework for higher education of the future. The knowledge explosion has made obsolete the faculty member who was only a classroom performer. It has compounded, too, the need for even more articulated teaching skills. Faculty members need to be teaching scholars -- properly equipped with effective teaching competencies and thorough knowledge of their disciplines. It is time to reflect on higher education as it was before the infusion of the German research university.

Attention must be given to some of the long-time examples of disciplinary teaching scholars as exemplified by Louis Agassiz, Benjamin Sillman, and Francis Wayland. For graduate education, this means changes in the doctoral programs to ensure that teaching strategies, course development skills, and evaluation techniques are integral aspects of one's preparation for a career in higher education. The future demands these new prerequisites for entry into the profession. It means that higher education institutions **must** require that prospective faculty members demonstrate both content and pedagogical competencies. Likewise, institutional changes must be forthcoming in the manner in which instruction is evaluated. The classroom must become an arena where the areas of content relevance and student progress are integrated and assessed. What better way to measure one's level of scholarship than regularly to assess it in day-to-day contacts with students? One's disciplinary competence must be added to the typical teaching assessment areas of course preparation, content organization, and classroom performances. Faculty evaluation then represents the marriage of scholarship and instructional effectiveness.

In a similar fashion, the professoriate must devise new approaches to the review and evaluation of scholarship. Again, the knowledge explosion has made obsolete the traditional means of assessing the professional competence of faculty members. For many, at the turn of the century a faculty member's authorship of a textbook demonstrated competence in one's discipline. An article or two may have covered an entire course. The knowledge explosion has made much of this conventional wisdom of evaluation obsolete. Today, individual competence across an entire discipline is rare and often an article is unrelated to one's general teaching assignment or may constitute only a small segment of a course. Furthermore, today's textbooks are typically less focused on scholarship than is a well developed research article. The current measures of scholarly excellence must be assessed and expanded. Clearly, one way to measure more fully one's professional competence is through the regular review of course materials and the assessment of how effectively these materials are used in classroom activities. Through this day-to-day review of disciplinary expertise, a more complete assessment of the teaching scholar's effectiveness can be made. Similarly, procedures which commonly involve a cursory review of scholarly materials must be greatly enhanced. The assessment process of professional competence includes more than measuring the number of juried articles/performances, the size of research grants, and the volume of materials produced.

---

*The unrealistic separation of teaching and scholarship and the duality of a reward system that pits one against the other do not present a workable framework for higher education of the future ... Faculty members need to be teaching scholars -- properly equipped with effective teaching competencies and thorough knowledge of their disciplines.*

---

The challenges of the decades ahead demand more than the outlined changes in the basic character of a faculty member, the full implementation of the teaching scholar concept, and the evaluation of the complete range of faculty competencies. Similar to the demands being placed on individuals in the academic community, administrators and institutions must also demonstrate a new level of commitment to teaching. Faculty must accurately evaluate colleague competence and performance. Committees must establish or modify employment, compensation, promotion, and tenure procedures so proper consideration can be given to the full range of factors that demonstrate professional competence. Support mechanisms and reward structures need to be modified so they respond to the changing demands being placed on individuals and institutions.

It will not be an easy task to move the higher education establishment toward these ideals. While support will come from many, the detractors and obstacles are formidable. The barriers will not crumble overnight. It seems apparent, however, that the profession has matured to the stage where it is ready to address this agenda. Maintenance of the status quo of promoting traditionally-defined research for most faculty members is like justifying college athletics for the sake of producing professional players. The various entities served by higher education and the academic community itself deserve more! A sense of priority and commitment to instructional effectiveness must become a reality.

---

*... the detractors and obstacles are formidable. The barriers will not crumble overnight. It seems apparent, however, that the profession has matured to the stage where it is ready to address this agenda.*

---

# Chapter Three
## INTEGRAL NATURE OF TEACHING

Research has been a part of American higher education since its introduction in the last quarter of the nineteenth century. Simultaneously, its ebb and flow has been the source of considerable controversy. For many faculty members, the publish-or-perish syndrome characterizes what is viewed as a disproportionate amount of attention given to the research aspect of their professional careers. Conventional wisdom suggests that many prestigious institutions are dominated by their commitment to research and that teaching and service activities are greatly diminished. The validity of this statement is subject, of course, to interpretation and varies from campus to campus and individual to individual. Attempts to portray teaching and research as separate entities or to criticize these relationships with broad, sweeping generalities seem frivolous. Rather, the academic community is better served by attempts that demonstrate the interrelationships between these two integral components of the educational process.

As a beginning point, thought needs to be given to the manner in which institutions are grouped and presented to the general public. Reference to an institution as a "research university", for example, is certainly a misnomer in terms of the institution's diversity, functions, expenditures of resources, and allocation of faculty time. The use of such verbal shorthand to characterize an institution as being of some higher order only serves to undercut the primary teaching mission of all institutions. Similarly, it perpetuates the perspective that research is the driving force of the university.

Even more fundamental to the integral nature of these institutional functions are the philosophical and operational understandings established by the academic community. How much better to speak of broadly defined scholarship rather than narrowly interpreted research! After all, the essence of a faculty member is scholarship -- the art of inquiry, discovery, and mastery. These activities have changed little over time. The condition under which faculty members perform and the expectations for them, however, are quite different today. It is these differences in responsibility that call for a rethinking of the relationships between scholarship and teaching.

Scholarship has long been a primary component in the maintenance of subject matter competence in a faculty member's chosen profession. The prescribed nature of expertise and its attendant components vary with each discipline. While there is considerable controversy over how one demonstrates and validates this competence, practicing one's art is fundamental to being a professor. The purposes of individual scholarship and its interrelationship with teaching must be clearly articulated. Faculty members must acknowledge this relationship and demonstrate its application. The traditional distinctions between teaching and research are no longer workable. The position of either/or cannot be tolerated within the dynamic nature of the profession. The scholarship continuum represents an enormous range of opportunities for faculty members. The practice of using scholarship as a means to maintain professional competence in one's discipline rests on one extreme. On the other end, is the pursuit of knowledge and those areas more narrowly defined by some as "pure research". Regardless of one's discipline, the option of having no scholarly activity is not a viable alternative for the present-day professional in higher education. To be productive, membership in the academic community requires that each faculty member be somewhere on the scholarship continuum.

---

*Regardless of one's discipline, the option of having no scholarly activity is not a viable alternative for the present-day professional in higher education. To be productive, membership in the academic community requires that each faculty member be somewhere on the scholarship continuum.*

---

The demands upon faculty members today, however, are far greater and more diverse than was the case when the research ingredient was first introduced into American higher education. For the most part, scholarship during these early years was more broadly conceived. Today, it is more common for one's expertise to be limited to a small portion of a course or to an area that may have little relevance to the content being taught by the individual. While the scholar's work might bring great prestige to the university (and often sizeable financial resources), a gap is often present between one's area of scholarship and the chosen teaching responsibilities.

Beyond the broadening knowledge base and the narrowing of faculty research interests are numerous other factors that suggest the need to integrate scholarship and teaching activities. The last century created a totally new learning environment in higher education. Many of the purposes of higher education have become focused more upon serving individual interests rather than providing for larger societal needs. Institutions have developed more diverse missions, and demands for increased accountability have been greatly expanded. The homogeneity of the student body has been replaced by a heterogeneous group with widely varying educational needs. The commonalities of the professoriate have been fractionalized into isolated compartments. While the maturing of the educational process has produced a rich body of knowledge encompassing teaching and learning theory, the role of the professor has shifted away from being a dispenser of knowledge to one that more frequently builds relationships and raises questions. Clearly, the expanded teaching roles, along with the other campus-wide demands, have placed tremendously broadened expectations upon the typical professor.

At a point in our nation's history, it was easier to make the case for a singular thrust in teaching or research. The pace of college life was different. The expectations of faculty were less and the public and students, in general, were far less demanding. While some faculty members long for the days when they felt that teaching was their only obligation, those days are gone. The knowledge explosion and needs of society have extended the need for continuous ongoing scholarship. The complexities of the modern-day campus have virtually eliminated the singularly-minded teaching professor. Gone, too, on most campuses is the position of the highly productive researcher who has little skill or time to fulfill teaching responsibilities. Economic and employment conditions do not allow that type of an assignment, and students do not tolerate such classroom incompetence. Recent as they may be, these changes suggest that the relationships between teaching and scholarship will be dramatically different in the decades ahead.

These changes have produced a fundamental shift in the basic teaching nature of the professoriate. Faculty members must demonstrate a broader knowledge over a widened content specialty. Delivery skills must be honed at a higher level of teaching expertise. Colleagues must have a greater understanding of their institution, its mission, and the clientele served. Faculty must be practicing scholars to maintain a state of the art commensurate with the title of professor. Most importantly, faculty members must stand ready to receive instructional criticism to the same extent they are willing to provide intellectual criticism.

---

*Faculty must be practicing scholars to maintain a state of the art commensurate with the title of professor. Most importantly, faculty members must stand ready to receive instructional criticism to the same extent they are willing to provide intellectual criticism.*

---

The expectations of today have produced conditions experienced by most faculty members that are far different than when they entered the profession in the sixties and seventies. These changes in the professional work environment (which often go unmentioned) provide added insights into many of the morale issues currently facing a large portion of the academic community. There are issues of salary, load, teaching conditions, etc. Of even greater consequence is the fact that if dramatic changes are not made, to recognize the emergence of the new expectations in higher education, the faculty's negative attitudes will continue to escalate. The entire academic community must recognize that the new burdens placed on faculty members require a bonding between teaching excellence and relevant scholarship. It is too easy to become comfortable with existing ideas, present perspectives, and today's classroom performance. Faculty must continuously study the discipline and practice its art. A professor must be a teacher. A teacher must be a learner constantly testing new insights on his/her peers, as well as students. Teaching, then, in its broadest sense, extends to students in the classroom, to colleagues throughout the campus community, and to scholars throughout the discipline. It is through this holistic view of the teaching/learning/scholarship process that the mutual goals and needs of both the students and faculty are achieved. For the faculty members of the future, the role of the teaching scholar naturally evolves. Research and other forms of scholarship complement the teaching function and vice versa.

In the 1984 faculty survey from the Carnegie Foundation, Burton Clark (3:85) reported that most of the professoriate has a basic interest in research.

> ... [O]nly those in lower liberal arts colleges and community colleges broke away from the rest of the professoriate in having little interest in research; even in those locales a third or so of the faculty claimed some interest in research. In the intensive teaching environments of the leading liberal arts colleges, as many as one out of four faculty reported leaning toward a primary research interest and seven out of ten claimed a research interest as well as a teaching commitment. Research is hard to keep out. Faculties want it; most institutions either want or have to allow for it. Making allowance for research, even encouraging it, remains "a mark of first-class practice."

Patricia Cross (5:5-7) suggests that there are numerous ways for the teaching and research functions to complement each other. An element that is commonly overlooked is the level of research that is conducted in the classroom.

> Few people criticize college professors for not knowing their subject matter, but many think they don't know much about teaching it to others. Research on teaching convinces many of us that content and process need to be joined in both research and practice.

> Research on teaching will be more productive if it recognizes that methods effective in teaching physics may not work in history ... Classroom research makes it possible for classroom teachers themselves to assess the quality of learning in their own classrooms. More powerfully yet, classroom research can become a collaborative effort, within and across departments, to determine whether aggregated teaching goals add up to a curriculum and how much of that curriculum students are buying.

> After considerable puzzlement and frustration over the difficulties of educating college professors about their common profession of teaching, I have reached

the conclusion that teachers in the disciplines will have to get involved in doing their own research on teaching to make it both credible and useful. Classroom research is thus not only a promising route to advancing knowledge, but to disseminating and using it as well.

Most educators know, too, that good teachers must be active learners themselves and model for students an active mind at work on significant intellectual tasks. Teaching, however, properly understood, is just as intellectually demanding as research. Rather than urging dedicated teachers to engage themselves in advanced disciplinary research, we might better encourage them to join teaching and research in the classroom, with their students as participants, through research on teaching and learning.

While the potential for classroom research is immense, the profession has managed to maintain a clear line of demarcation between the formal qualities of the disciplines and the practices associated with its delivery. For the most part, the "acceptable definition" of research has remained discipline-oriented and relatively pure while the applied nature of the teaching/learning process has been set aside. Again, the opportunity is present to integrate scholarship and teaching. This task will not be easy; the forces that have traditionally separated teaching and scholarship are well ingrained into the very fabric of higher education. Eble (7:72) suggests, however, that there is hope, latent as it may be, in the central tendencies of the profession.

Teaching itself, for all the lamenting about its being valued less than scholarship, exerts a claim upon the majority of professors that helps explain the decline in scholarly productivity that accompanies rising in rank. The necessity of carrying out mandatory scheduled activities, the social aspects of teaching, and the clear superiority one enjoys over students as contrasted with editors of scholarly journals argue for giving teaching the in-fact priority. A day's work done, the strength to turn to the typewriter or return to the laboratory is simply not there for the majority. There is no mystery in this, nor should there be much guilt.

To move in this direction, the profession must be willing to bring a new level of sophistication to the validation processes for measuring effective scholarship and effective teaching. Before inroads can be made in the reward systems, it is imperative that the intellectual capacities of the academic community be concentrated on the construction of information and data bases that support clear cut decision-making processes on the effectiveness of instruction. This major demand must be addressed. The importance of teaching deserves more than an occasional colleague's visit and the collection of some student input.

Some of the artificial distinctions between teaching and research will likely lessen with the new generation of young scholars. Signs of this evolutionary process are already present as these neophytes are regularly employed with greater teaching promise, broader disciplinary competencies, and greater research skills that generally exceed the levels present in the profession. While the changing of the guard might exacerbate the elimination of traditional distinctions, this general phenomenon is characteristic of a maturing of the profession that is likely to continue in the years ahead.

The real agenda must come from within the academic community. Experts agree this will be no easy task. The philosophical underpinning of combining research and teaching is deeply ingrained in the American academic consciousness. The vast majority of academics across the nation want to do some research, publish a little, and maintain teaching as their first love. For the most part, the system is not designed to support, reward, or promote this type of behavior. Faculty members must assume an integral role in bringing about this change, but the fundamental leadership responsibility for the reorientation process must emerge from the administrators in the nation's colleges and universities. While some would exhort this change to occur overnight in a revolutionary manner, the likelihood of this occurrence is remote. In reality, however, a substantive shift of this magnitude can only occur in an evolutionary manner. As a matter of fact, the necessary elements to integrate teaching and scholarship are not in place. Work needs to be completed on various employment procedures, evaluative alternatives, reward systems, and most importantly, the attitudes that prevail in major segments of the profession.

As this process moves forward, it can be expected that some individuals will automatically jump to the extreme. In defense of the status quo, they will contend that what is being suggested is to make teaching the overriding component in American higher education. The argument will proceed that such a ridiculous move would be the downfall of our present-day system and would make the college teaching profession more like school teaching. Concerns will be expressed that the system will lose the diversity and flexibility so integral to its distinctive nature. To the contrary, higher education must have significant research efforts and great scholarly achievements. Institutions can and should place their priorities on those elements that best support their particular missions. In the classroom, the profession cannot accept an either/or posture. The integral nature of teaching and scholarship must be firmly intertwined. Ernest Boyer (6:131) vividly illustrated this point in his recent book **College: The Undergraduate Experience in America** when he noted the differences between the institution and the individual.

> ... [H]ere an important distinction should be drawn. While not all professors are or should be publishing researchers, they, nonetheless, should be first-rate scholars. We understand this to mean staying abreast of the profession, knowing the literature in one's field, and skillfully communicating such information to students. To weaken faculty commitment to scholarship, as we define it here, is to undermine the undergraduate experience, regardless of the academic setting.

> Further, the results of such scholarship should be made available for judgment. There are many ways to do this: Apart from publishing books, monographs, or articles in journals, a scholar can write textbooks, participate in conferences, develop new approaches to instruction, and, most especially, be more effective in the classroom. In one or a combination of these ways, such activities should be evaluated by peers. How else can we judge whether a faculty member is staying professionally alive?

This is the point: Scholarship is not an esoteric appendage; it is at the heart of what the profession is all about. All faculty, throughout their careers, should, themselves, remain students. As scholars, they must continue to learn and be seriously and continuously engaged in the expanding intellectual world.

The complex scholarly process deserves more than just the review of the number of presentations, publications, grants, and awards. The absence of developing sound evaluative approaches leaves the college teaching profession at the mercy of those who continue to promote the dichotomy between teaching and research. Simply put, if the profession will not effectively evaluate the totality of teaching and devise alternative modes to assess all aspects of scholarship, the professoriate will abdicate its professional responsibility in favor of a mere counting of publications and grants. Surely, the future of teaching and learning in our colleges and universities deserves more.

A realistic appraisal of each discipline demonstrates the point that only through the evaluation of teaching can one fully assess the scholarly competence of an individual. The complexity of knowledge renders it impossible for an article or two to validate one's competence in the discipline. Daily teaching contacts, however, provide countless opportunities for faculty members to demonstrate their scholarship -- the introduction of new insights/research can be tested, the development of new materials can be evaluated, the relevancy of curriculum initiatives can be assessed, and the appropriateness of content can be measured. Simultaneously, the actual preparation, organization, and presentation skills of teaching can be judged.

---

*Simply put, if the profession will not effectively evaluate the totality of teaching and devise alternative modes to assess all aspects of scholarship, the professoriate will abdicate its professional responsibility in favor of a mere counting of publications and grants.*

---

The challenge to strengthen teaching must be accepted by the administrators on campuses across the nation. The initiative, the push, and the sustained effort must be unmistakably clear. A statement of priority for teaching must be made. Policies, procedures, and actions must reveal this commitment. The academy needs to reaffirm the role of the teaching scholar. The artificial dichotomy between scholarly activity and teaching must be dismantled, and the commonalities between the two must become a new focal point. The connections and reinforcing agents must be drawn out and emphasized. Then, bold steps must be taken to move higher education back in touch with the professional expectations of faculty members and the educational needs of students.

# Chapter Four

## STATUS OF COLLEGE TEACHING

The challenges to elevate the status of teaching are massive and require a sustained level of action over a prolonged period of time. While the need for effective instruction at all levels of education (K-college) has gained the nation's attention, this initiative cannot achieve its highest goals without direct intervention by administrators in the nation's higher education institutions. The increased levels of interest and rhetoric about teaching present an opportunity for change that is unmatched in this century. Administrators across the nation have an obligation to seize the opportunity. They must assume a leadership posture that forces individuals throughout higher education to rethink their basic attitudes about teaching and how to recognize, reward, and promote it. Action must be taken to reassess existing structures and devise new approaches to support a higher level of commitment to college teaching.

This leadership challenge is complex and cannot be accomplished by a singular action or in a haphazard fashion. Substantive reform requires a calculated change initiative that is coherently planned, organized, and implemented. The initiative requires broad-based support and involvement of the various constituencies throughout higher education. Administrators and faculty members need to work together to achieve mutually acceptable goals. Individual biases need to be set aside so efforts can be directed toward constructive solutions that enhance instructional effectiveness on campus. Action needs to be taken to appraise current campus attitudes and perceptions; review existing policies and procedures; and construct a practical structure that will maintain a high level of commitment to teaching.

Fundamental to these efforts is the development of a research base that provides a means for campus analysis and nationwide comparison. The questions that must be asked present the professoriate with unmatched opportunities to probe and research the various instructional structures of higher education. For example, what are the various approaches that might be used to assess one's intellectual vitality? How can instructional effectiveness be assessed in terms of student outcomes? What evaluative strategies may be used to demonstrate instructional effectiveness? What models can be developed to firmly connect teaching and learning? What reward structures are needed to instill the primacy of teaching?

---

*This leadership challenge is complex and cannot be accomplished by a singular action or in a haphazard fashion. Substantive reform requires a calculated change initiative that is coherently planned, organized, and implemented.*

---

In the fall of 1987, as an initial step in the process, the author undertook a national survey of chief academic officers in the nation's four-year degree granting institutions. The research was designed to collect base-line data on the existing level of commitment to instructional effectiveness and to suggest areas that deserve attention so substantive changes could be made in the instructional patterns of the nation's colleges and universities. The study was based on a review of literature that identified important elements that were supportive of or promoted effective teaching. The identified twenty-five items in the final instrument were distributed equally under five major headings of employment policies and practices, campus environment and culture, strategic administrative actions, instructional enhancement efforts, and instructional development activities (see Appendix A). The research instrument was then sent to over two thousand chief academic officers of four-year colleges and universities throughout the nation who were listed in the U.S. Office of Education mailing list (HEGIS XIX). Seventy-five surveys were dropped from the study for self-exclusion reasons or because they were returned as unopened mail. The population size was determined to be 2028. There was 1046 (51.6%) responses to the first mailing in October 1987. A second mailing in December 1987 increased the total usable responses to 1328 (65.4%).

To determine whether the respondent group of 1328 chief academic officers represented a random sampling of the HEGIS XIX population, Chi Square tests (pr $>0.01$) of sample deviation from known characteristics were performed for the institutions. The eight variables tested were regional accreditation, control or affiliation, highest level of offerings, institutional control, land-grant status, enrollment, undergraduate tuition, and required fees. For purposes of the analysis, enrollment was categorized by quintile. Private and in-state undergraduate tuition and required fees were categorized by quartile, according to the distribution of the variables in the population of the 2028 institutions.

The 1328 respondents were considered as a random sample of the total survey population on the characteristics of regional accreditation, highest level of offerings, institutional control, land grant status, private undergraduate tuition and required fees, and in-state tuition and required fees. The sample and population differed in regard to control or affiliation, with relatively fewer independent, nonprofit institutions responding and relatively more state institutions responding. The sample also differed by enrollment, with relatively fewer small institutions (less than 404) responding (pr >0.01). Since these two variables often test for the same elements, it is estimated that approximately twenty additional respondents from the smallest group of institutions would have been needed to provide a true random sample of the population in all characteristics. For comparative purposes, Table 4 presents an overview of the composition of the respondents in the survey.

The findings from this survey were analyzed from three different perspectives. First, in the next section of this chapter, the composite scores for each of the five major categories are presented. These arrays provide an overall context in which instructional effectiveness can be assessed. Second, the attitudes of the chief academic officers in terms of their levels of satisfaction with institutional performance and personal attention are presented in the final portion of this chapter. This analysis suggests the extent to which academic leaders are comfortable with the current status of teaching on their campuses. Third, each of the five major categories is more thoroughly analyzed in Chapters 5 through 9. In each case, emphasis is placed on the data collected for the individual items and the comments received from the respondents. Since enrollment was the only one of the eight variables that consistently revealed significant differences between institutional responses, it, too, receives special attention.

## Table 4
## Composition of Respondents in the National Survey
## (From HEGIS XIX 1984-1985)

| Variable                                      Values | Response # | Rate % |
|------------------------------------------------------|------------|--------|
| Regional Accreditations                              |            |        |
| New England Association of Schools & Colleges        | 97         | 63%    |
| Middle States Association of Schools & Colleges      | 228        | 62%    |
| North Central Association of Colleges &              |            |        |
|   Secondary Schools                        | 445        | 76%    |
| Northwest Association of Schools & Colleges          | 58         | 74%    |
| Southern Association of Colleges & Schools           | 302        | 71%    |
| Western Association of Schools & Colleges            | 78         | 59%    |
| Other or Missing                                     | 120        | 43%    |
|   Total                                    | 1,328      | 65%    |
|                                                      |            |        |
| Control of Affiliation                               |            |        |
| Independent Non-Profit                               | 395        | 57%    |
| State                                                | 394        | 74%    |
| Other                                                | 539        | 67%    |
|   Total                                    | 1,328      | 65%    |
|                                                      |            |        |
| Highest Level of Offering                            |            |        |
| Doctorate                                            | 268        | 58%    |
| First-Professional and Master's                      | 560        | 70%    |
| Four or Five Year Baccalaureate                      | 492        | 69%    |
|   Total                                    | 1,320      | 67%    |
|                                                      |            |        |
| Institution Control                                  |            |        |
| Public                                               | 418        | 73%    |
| Private                                              | 909        | 63%    |
|   Total                                    | 1,328      | 65%    |
|                                                      |            |        |
| Land Grant Status                                    |            |        |
| Non-Land Grant Institution                           | 1,169      | 66%    |
| Land Grant Institution                               | 48         | 65%    |
| Member of NASULGC                                    | 75         | 71%    |
|                                                      |            |        |
| Enrollment (By Quintile)                             |            |        |
| 1st  Quintile of Population (1-404)                  | 198        | 50%    |
| 2nd Quintile of Population (405-976)                 | 268        | 67%    |
| 3rd  Quintile of Population (977-2,011)              | 266        | 67%    |
| 4th  Quintile of Population (2,012-5,661)            | 300        | 75%    |
| 5th  Quintile of Population (over 5,661)             | 275        | 69%    |
|   Total                                    | 1,307      | 66%    |

**Table 4 Cont.**

| | | |
|---|---|---|
| Private Undergraduate Tuition and Required Fees | | |
| 1st  Quarter of Population ($3,085.00 or less) | 174 | 56% |
| 2nd Quarter of Population ($3,085.01 - $4,408.50) | 211 | 69% |
| 3rd  Quarter of Population ($4,408.51 - $5,650.00) | 218 | 71% |
| 4th  Quarter of Population (over $5,650.01) | 200 | 65% |
| Total | 803 | 65% |
| | | |
| In-State Undergraduate Tuition and Required Fees | | |
| 1st  Quarter of Population ($815.50 or less) | 95 | 69% |
| 2nd Quarter of Population (815.51 - $1,104.00) | 110 | 80% |
| 3rd  Quarter of Population ($1,104.01 - $1,454.00) | 100 | 72% |
| 4th  Quarter of Population (over  $1,454.00) | 95 | 69% |
| Total | 400 | 73% |

## Commitment to Instructional Effectiveness

To assess the overall commitment to instructional effectiveness, the chief academic officers rated the twenty-five items on a scale of 1 (low) to 10 (high). In each case, the academic officers were asked to assess the extent to which these factors affected the campus instructional program.

A general analysis of their perceptions reveals that there are significant differences in the levels of institutional commitment within the five sub-areas. These distinctions are particularly noteworthy, since they vividly illustrate that efforts made to enhance the level of commitment to teaching must be appropriately tailored action by action and campus to campus. Different levels of activity will be needed if a campus is to implement effectively the desired reforms.

The overall data from the study indicate the broad generalizations to re-emphasize teaching or singular efforts to "change the system" will not likely create the type of reform that will be needed. Changing the level of commitment to teaching is a more complex task than it may appear on the surface. The typical rhetoric from administrators to place more emphasis on teaching or the demands from faculty members for greater rewards will not accomplish the desired goals. Efforts that are diverse in nature and sustained over a long period of time will be required to elevate effectively the importance of teaching.

*Changing the level of commitment to teaching is a more complex task than it may appear on the surface. The typical rhetoric from administrators to place more emphasis on teaching or the demands from faculty members for greater rewards will not accomplish the desired goals.*

Table 5 presents a breakdown of the general perceptions of the chief academic officers regarding instructional effectiveness. These tabulations were calculated by summing the responses from the five items under each of the categories. (The highest possible score for each category would be 50 if each item were rated as a 10.) The area

**Table 5**
**The Perceptions of Chief Academic Officers for the Five Major Categories by Size of Institution**

| Institutional Enrollment | Sample Size | Employ Policy | Campus Culture | Strategic Action | Enhance Effort | Devel. Activity |
|---|---|---|---|---|---|---|
| < 200 | 102 | 32.6 | 39.3 | 24.2 | 26.0 | 14.9 |
| 200 - 499 | 139 | 34.0 | 37.2 | 26.6 | 26.6 | 15.5 |
| 500 - 999 | 233 | 39.5 | 36.8 | 29.9 | 28.5 | 18.2 |
| 1000 - 2499 | 342 | 41.5 | 36.8 | 30.5 | 29.7 | 17.8 |
| 2500 - 4999 | 188 | 41.9 | 35.8 | 30.9 | 31.1 | 19.1 |
| 5000 - 9999 | 145 | 41.6 | 35.6 | 30.5 | 30.2 | 20.7 |
| 10000 - 19999 | 114 | 42.2 | 36.3 | 31.3 | 31.0 | 23.7 |
| 20000 - Over | 48 | 40.5 | 35.8 | 32.8 | 30.1 | 27.5 |
| **Mean Composite Score** | | **39.6** | **36.7** | **29.7** | **29.2** | **18.8** |

of employment policies and practices includes statements regarding employment, promotion, tenure, student evaluation, and recognition programs. Under campus environment and culture, the items included were institutional pride, administrative stability, administrative leadership, morale on campus, and faculty ownership of the curriculum. The category of strategic administrative actions was defined by items that stressed the importance of teaching, use of news releases, role of research on campus, and the collection of data on teaching. Instructional enhancement efforts included the promotion of teaching through the use of librarians, released time, financial support, curriculum development initiatives, and scholarship.

The final area of instructional development gave attention to workshops, seminars, conferences, support mechanisms, and development activities on campus.

A general inspection of the sums presented in Table 5 reveals several important observations. First, the category of employment policies and practices is judged as the area with the highest level of institutional commitment. The lowest level of institutional support was instructional development activities. Second, institutional enrollment differences have a significant impact on the perceived level of commitment to instructional effectiveness. Larger institutions, for example, appear to devote far more attention to instructional development activities than do their smaller counterparts. Third, there is a modest increase in the use of instructional enhancement and strategic administrative actions to support teaching as one progresses toward the larger institutions. Fourth, the integral role of teaching in various employment practices tends to increase with institutional size until enrollment reaches about 20,000 and then declines modestly. Fifth, the extent to which the campus environment supports a strong commitment to teaching tends to decline as the campus gets larger.

## Levels of Satisfaction With
## Institutional Performance

One of the most important factors in any reform initiative is to determine the level of satisfaction or uneasiness experienced by those who must assume a major leadership role in the change process. If leaders are, in fact, happy or pleased with the current situation, the likelihood of their advocating change is greatly diminished. Conversely, a relatively high level of administrative discontentment may suggest a high level of readiness to press forward with substantial modification of existing patterns.

The data from the 1300+ chief academic officers suggest that several areas exist where their level of satisfaction is quite low. In fact, even in the highest rated area, employment policies and practices, the 7.7 mean score on a ten-point scale is not overpowering. Table 6 presents the percentage of chief academic officers' ratings of the five categories according to their grouping on the ten-point rating scale. It indicates, for example, that 14% of the academic leaders gave the employment policies and practices category a rating of 10, whereas only 2% gave instructional development activities a 10 rating. The clustering of double digit percentage responses further illustrates the descending level of satisfaction with the five areas.

**Table 6**
**Ratings of Chief Academic Officers' Satisfaction Levels with Institutional Performance by Instructional Improvement Category**

| Category | Percentage by Level of Rating | | | | | | | | | | Mean |
|---|---|---|---|---|---|---|---|---|---|---|---|
| | 1 | 2 | 3 | 4 | 5 | 6 | 7 | 8 | 9 | 10 | |
| Employment Policies and Practices | 1 | 1 | 2 | 4 | 6 | 8 | 13 | 27 | 25 | 14 | 7.7 |
| Campus Environment and Culture | 1 | 1 | 3 | 4 | 9 | 13 | 20 | 25 | 16 | 8 | 7.1 |
| Strategic Administrative Actions | 1 | 3 | 5 | 7 | 11 | 14 | 19 | 22 | 14 | 5 | 6.7 |
| Instructional Enhancement Efforts | 3 | 5 | 10 | 11 | 14 | 13 | 17 | 18 | 7 | 3 | 5.8 |
| Instructional Development Activities | 6 | 9 | 14 | 12 | 11 | 11 | 17 | 13 | 5 | 2 | 5.2 |

The 7.7 mean score in the employment policies and practices category presents the higher education community with an interesting anomaly. While chief academic officers give this area their highest level of satisfaction rating, faculty members typically identify promotion and tenure as the biggest deterrents to making teaching a more viable institutional function. This apparent disparity raises several important questions. For example, will academic administrators vigorously support faculty initiatives to elevate the importance of teaching in those tangible areas of employment, promotion, tenure, and recognition? Or, does their rating suggest that most chief academic officers believe that the procedures are already in place? Will administrators be more interested in making changes first in other categories? Regardless of the response, the 7.7 rating reveals that there is significant opportunity to make changes in this area. The high level of faculty criticism that is generally communicated in this category may be used as a compelling force for change.

A quick perusal of Table 6 also illustrates that the level of satisfaction is only moderately high for the campus environment and culture category. The level of positive support for the other categories is substantially less. If one were to use a rating of 8 and above to generally suggest a desired, good/excellent rating, the low levels of satisfaction would be even more obvious. The percentage of chief academic officers who rated the categories at the good/excellent levels was as follows: Employment Policies and Practices -- 66%; Campus Environment and Culture -- 49%; Strategic Administrative Actions -- 41%; Instructional Enhancement Efforts -- 28%; and Instructional Development Activities -- 20%. While not presented in Table 6, it is interesting to note that the ratings of the chief academic officers remain relatively consistent regardless of the size of institution they represent. Only in the instructional development category did chief academic officers tend to give slightly higher ratings at the larger than at smaller institutions (5.7 vs. 4.7). Clearly, the opportunity for strong aggressive leadership is great in all areas. Each of the areas presents significant opportunities for substantial improvements. As a general observation, many of these areas of opportunity represent changes that could be made with relatively few new costs. For the most part, the changes require a strong administrative commitment and the dedication of large amounts of time and energy.

---

*The percentage of chief academic officers who rated the categories at the good/excellent levels was as follows: Employment Policies and Practices -- 66%; Campus Environment and Culture -- 49%; Strategic Administrative Actions -- 41%; Instructional Enhancement Efforts -- 28%; and Instructional Development Activities -- 20%.*

---

## Levels of Satisfaction with Personal Attention

Chief academic officers were also asked to assess their level of satisfaction with the amount of personal attention they devote to these five instructional improvement categories. Table 7 presents these findings in the same format as used in Table 6. It is not surprising to find that academic leaders express a relatively low level of satisfaction with the amount of personal attention they devote to the promotion of teaching. There is a high level of readiness for change among these academic leaders in the nation. Their time and energy commitments in support of the teaching function are less than might be desired. While their personal assessments are slightly higher than their assessment of their institutions, the percentages in the 8 and above columns closely parallel their institutional satisfaction levels. The percentage of academic officers that place the five categories at the good/excellent level is as follows: Employment Policies and Practices -- 65%; Campus Environment and Culture -- 53%; Strategic Administrative Actions -- 54%; Instructional Enhancement Efforts -- 34%; and Instructional Development Activities -- 28%. Again, the variation in the attitudes of chief academic officers at institutions of varying size is quite small. Attitudes concerning the campus environment and culture, and strategic administrative actions were essentially constant across all groups. Employment policies and practices were rated slightly higher (8.0) at institutions in the 1000 - 9999 range, while other groupings clustered around the 7.6 level. In the instructional enhancement and instructional development categories, the perceptions of chief academic officers were slightly stronger at larger institutions. (In the case of instructional enhancement, the mean at smaller institutions was 6.0 vs. 6.8 for larger institutions. For development activities, the mean at smaller institutions was 5.5 vs. 6.7 for larger institutions.)

### Table 7
### Ratings of Chief Academic Officers' Satisfaction Levels
### with Amount of Personal Attention
### Devoted to the Instructional Improvement Categories

| Category | Percentage by Level of Rating | | | | | | | | | | Mean |
|---|---|---|---|---|---|---|---|---|---|---|---|
| | 1 | 2 | 3 | 4 | 5 | 6 | 7 | 8 | 9 | 10 | |
| Employment Policies and Practices | 1 | 1 | 2 | 4 | 6 | 7 | 13 | 23 | 24 | 18 | 7.8 |
| Campus Environment and Culture | 0 | 1 | 3 | 4 | 9 | 11 | 18 | 24 | 19 | 10 | 7.4 |
| Strategic Administrative Actions | 0 | 2 | 3 | 5 | 8 | 11 | 17 | 21 | 20 | 13 | 7.3 |
| Instructional Enhancement Efforts | 2 | 5 | 8 | 10 | 11 | 14 | 16 | 19 | 10 | 5 | 6.2 |
| Instructional Development Activities | 4 | 8 | 10 | 11 | 11 | 13 | 15 | 15 | 9 | 4 | 5.7 |

*It is not surprising to find that academic leaders express a relatively low level of satisfaction with the amount of personal attention they devote to the promotion of teaching. There is a high level of readiness for change among these academic leaders in the nation.*

A typical comment made by academic leaders in addressing this part of the research was that they have little time to devote to the fundamental functions of the institution. Those "areas that are so important, like teaching, do not receive the appropriate level of attention because they are seldom elevated to the crisis level." Whether or not this is the reason, their attitudes certainly represent a less than satisfactory rating of the amount of personal attention given to the major areas that support teaching. The "happiness quotient" represented by the range of means from 5.7 to 7.8 leaves considerable opportunity for improvement.

The extent to which one's level of satisfaction parallels one's willingness to change or improve a situation may be debated, but the data suggest that there are numerous opportunities to bring about immediate change. Outside the employment policies and practices category, most of the burden for change falls directly or indirectly on the shoulders of the academic administrators of the institution. Furthermore, most of these areas do not require changes in policy or legislative action by a faculty body. The type of changes being called for, however, do require 1) a firm expression of the importance of teaching; 2) a willingness to marshal resources to support excellence in the classroom; 3) an ability to lead a campus-wide initiative to change existing attitudes, perceptions, and, in some cases, procedures; 4) an ability to build bonds and linkages between administrative personnel and faculty colleagues; and 5) a willingness to develop a plan of action that provides the basis for a consistent and sustained campus-wide effort. The opportunity for substantive change is squarely before the academic community; the leadership challenge must be accepted by academic leaders across the nation!

*The opportunity for substantive change is squarely before the academic community; the leadership challenge must be accepted by academic leaders across the nation!*

# Chapter Five

## CAMPUS ENVIRONMENT AND CULTURE

The topics of organizational climate, culture, and environment have long been areas of intellectual pursuit in the field of business. The last two decades, however, have witnessed a substantial growth in the volume of literature dedicated to these aspects of organizational structure and behavior. The last five years have seen a marked increase in such studies within higher education. **The Organization Context for Teaching and Learning** published by the National Center for Research to Improve Postsecondary Teaching and Learning provides a recent comprehensive review of research in these areas.

The perspectives of writers regarding organizational culture vary widely and present differing views on how the environment and climate affect basic corporate functions. For higher education, it is clear that there is an "institutional quality of life" that influences faculty attitudes and actions. Such factors obviously affect the overall quality of instruction provided by the campus. Every campus has tangible structures, verifiable behaviors, and measurable group and individual attitudes that shape actions taken and decisions made about the institution. A paper by Edwin Fenton (10) from Carnegie Mellon University entitled "Developing a Culture of Teaching in a Small Research University" serves as an excellent example of how an institution might move forward in its efforts to shape or enhance the campus teaching environment.

The campus environment may be shaped by a variety of factors. Printed materials and formal communications present an impression or can form an image. Administrative actions and leadership styles can establish an overall campus tone. Institutional history and long standing traditions and habits can have a bearing on the campus culture. As one chief academic officer from a midwestern comprehensive university noted, the context for change resulting from a negative situation can be particularly narrowing.

> The culture here has developed over an extended period and will change significantly only with time (and retirement). I could write virtually a dissertation on that statement, but will not attempt to go into such detail. I might give you one or two examples of what I mean.

> First, there was a long period of oppression under a prior administration. Many faculty continue to relate to administrators as well as to each other, under the cycle of fear they experienced for almost twenty years. It simply will not matter how open new administrations might be or how willing faculty colleagues will be for intellectual exchange. These faculty have been trained under the old regime for far too many years to change many of their behaviors. Consequently, the culture of suspicion will not disappear until these faculty disappear themselves or become so few that their impact is diminished.

> As a second example, we have a number of people in teacher education who have always followed the public school model and done such things as paint houses as soon as they could get out of class. It is very doubtful that we will ever be able to use evaluation, or any other vehicle, to change the behavior of these faculty.This not only impacts on their efforts directed toward teacher education, but also impacts upon the perception of other faculty on campus about teacher education. Again, this will not be solved until certain people retire. There is one bright spot -- we have already begun to pick up a few of the resignations, with noticeable results in the culture of at least a few departments.

On the other hand, the fundamental ingredients of academic planning may be used to develop a strong teaching commitment. The goal/objective setting approach used at Southeast Missouri State University includes a regular communication of action and an open sharing of information and illustrates one way to elevate the importance of teaching excellence. One of eight major academic goals and supporting objectives for the 1985-90 planning cycle focused on teaching:

## Achieve Greater Teaching Effectiveness and Promote Other Activities Which Increase Learning and Demonstrate Quality Education

Increase efforts to encourage learning and strengthen activities designed to improve the quality of instruction.

Seek means by which outstanding teaching and learning are recognized and rewarded systematically throughout the University. (e.g. merit)

Encourage and support extensive study and implementation of outcome measures in university programs to demonstrate quality education.

Increase scholarship/research activities that strengthen the teaching process and support the University's primary commitment to teaching and learning excellence.

Continue to support inservice seminars and workshops for teaching renewal and enhancement through the Center for Teaching and Learning. Encourage active faculty involvement with continuous renewal of their teaching in conjunction with the Center.

Further develop the University-wide system for the evaluation of teaching effectiveness through the development of outcome measures.

While conditions vary on every campus, the administration has the obligation to demonstrate efforts that shape campus attitudes, influence campus leaders, and produce conditions supportive of excellence in the classroom. The initiatives may be formal or informal, communicated by example or policy. Regardless of the mode, sustained actions must be taken.

*... the administration has the obligation to demonstrate efforts that shape campus attitudes, influence campus leaders, and produce conditions supportive of excellence in the classroom.*

## Supportive Nature of the Campus Environment and Culture

On a daily basis, numerous factors impinge upon the development of a positive campus environment. All too often, what typically gets attention on most campuses are negative events, actions, or rumors. Concerns over enrollment, resources, promotion and tenure, and a multitude of distracting elements often force teaching excellence to go unnoticed by many administrators. These issues are compounded by the very nature of a faculty member, who through personal efforts to analyze, probe, and question, seems to perpetuate this negative tendency. The creation of a positive teaching/learning environment requires constant attention.

Fortunately, the campus environment is typically a product of more long-term developments and is somewhat less susceptible to the immediate fluctuations of a few members within the culture than might be true for smaller segments within the institution. Beyond the classroom and the competency of the individual faculty member, there are several indicators that may be used to assess the general conduciveness of the campus teaching environment. One's level of security, sense of institutional pride, personal ownership in campus activities, perceptions about administrative leadership, and one's intellectual vitality all contribute to this sense of community. Faculty responses to a few basic questions can also suggest the overall tone of the campus: Does the campus have stability in its leadership team? Do the campus structures provide for open debate and dialogue? Is there a sense of faculty ownership in the curriculum? Is there a high level of pride in the institution's academic standards, and a strong commitment to students, quality of teaching and scholarship, and its programs? Are there research, scholarly, and creative activities under way that stimulate classroom instruction?

In an attempt to address issues of this type, chief academic officers in the study responded to five statements. Table 8 provides the overall group ratings and mean scores from this national sample. As a group of statements, the level of commitment to campus

## Table 8
## Perceived Commitment of the Campus Environment
## and Culture in Support of Instructional Effectiveness

| Items | % Rating 1,2 or 3 | Mean | % Rating 8,9 or 10 |
|---|---|---|---|
| Faculty have a clear sense of ownership of the curriculum and other instructional concerns | 2 | **8.3** | 74 |
| There is a shared feeling of institutional pride that stimulates effective classroom performance | 5 | **7.4** | 56 |
| The level of intellectual vitality and morale on campus is conducive to effective instruction | 3 | **7.3** | 53 |
| There is a clear sense of administrative stability that allows faculty to focus on the instructional process | 8 | **7.1** | 53 |
| The faculty have a clear sense of confidence in the upper administrative leadership that fosters effective instruction | 7 | **6.9** | 43 |

environment and culture ranked second highest to employment practices out of the five categories in the study. The item regarding faculty ownership of the curriculum (mean = 8.3) ranked as the fourth highest item out of the twenty-five statements. Seventy-four percent of the chief academic officers placed this item in the good/excellent category rating of 8, 9, or 10. This is the only item in this category that was within the good/excellent range (8 or above). While all of the items in this group ranked in the upper half of those surveyed, the mean scores of 6.9 and 7-plus reveal that across the nation there is only a moderately positive environment for sustaining the primary function of teaching. Only about half of the chief academic officers (53% and 56%) placed these items in the good/excellent category. These perceptions present numerous challenges for the professoriate. For example, what steps could be taken to minimize the effects of the negative forces impacting higher education? How can feelings of institutional pride, intellectual vitality, and involvement in campus operations be used to enhance teaching?

*One's level of security, sense of institutional pride, personal ownership in campus activities, perceptions about administrative leadership, and one's intellectual vitality all contribute to this sense of community.*

What campus actions are needed to stimulate greater instructional effectiveness, instill higher levels of administrative confidence, and facilitate greater administrative stability?

A partial answer to these and other questions is provided by a more thorough analysis of the views of the chief academic officers in the study. In the sections that follow, each of the five surveyed items is analyzed according to institutional size. Comments, insights, and examples collected in the research are also provided to amplify the specific perceptions.

## Administrative Ability

The importance of providing a consistent message, maintaining a constant level of commitment, and providing a continuous sense of direction are obvious needs for sustaining any initiative. This is particularly true with respect to teaching since its routine nature commonly leaves it in the "assumed category." Consequently, the importance of teaching is often highly susceptible to the perceived priorities or agendas of a new chief executive or academic officer. Chart 1 illustrates the general perception of chief academic officers that significant improvements in the teaching environment could be achieved by greater administrative stability. This perception is fairly consistent throughout the academic community. While there is a somewhat stronger sense of confidence in administrative stability at smaller institutions, this is an area in which overall improvement

**Chart 1**
**Impact of Administrative Stability on**
**Institutional Effectiveness by Size of Institution**

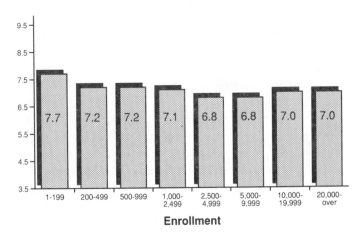

**Enrollment**

could enhance the conduciveness of the campus teaching environment.

There are many tentacles attached to the impact of administrative stability on instructional effectiveness. The academic vice president at a major southern institution noted that "political strife on campus has undermined efforts to focus attention on instructional effectiveness." The dean of instruction at a small religious college pointed out that "financial pressures and administrative instability have led to poor efforts aimed at improving teaching effectiveness." At a western regional university, the academic vice president indicated that "we are in a position of transition. The top three academic officers are all new to the campus this year. Morale has been bad, but we expect to turn it around." Another academic dean at a small midwestern college illustrated the often compounding nature of the problems -- "we do not have a large number of administrators, we're in a state of financial distress, and we have gone through two very comprehensive self-studies during the past years."

## Ideas for Action

The moderately positive ratings and supporting comments of the chief academic officers illustrate the need for strong leadership to improve the sense of faculty security and administrative stability. Some thoughts for initial action include such items as:

- Establish teaching as the institution's first priority and make appropriate commitments so its status won't waiver or be in dispute with new administrative appointments or academic agendas -- place strong emphasis on teaching in mission statements, lists of academic objectives, and budget funding priorities.

- Reduce the amount of institutional attention given to factors that tend to detract from academic priorities -- deal with budget concerns in a timely fashion, address parking problems, and make decisions on items that tend to distract the campus.

- Identify and improve those areas that directly affect the immediate teaching environment -- remodel and upgrade classrooms and laboratories, improve faculty offices, and provide computers and other types of up-to-date equipment.

- Maintain an open environment that removes procedural barriers, reduces faculty isolation, and promotes academic dialogue -- use procedures to promote rather than destroy change initiatives, share information widely, and create forums for open debate.

- Recognize the evolutionary nature of change and the importance of faculty ownership when mounting new initiatives -- take small steps that improve the environment,utilize faculty-based ideas, and compromise on procedures but not on principles.

- Provide academic leaders with a clear sense of campus needs and properly inform the campus of administrative expectations -- issue term appointments (e.g., five years), identify specified sets of expectations, and state planned directions.

## Faculty Ownership

Like almost all professionals, faculty members exhibit strong tendencies to be an integral part of their institution. In fact, their high levels of preparation and specialized competencies may make this statement truer for faculty than for any other group of professionals. There are, however, forces that naturally work against these normal instincts. Disciplinary and departmental pressures push faculty members to pursue narrow perspectives. The competitive nature of grants and research sometimes motivates faculty members toward pursuing personal rather than collaborative goals. The sheer size of some universities promotes the development of subcultures. Yet, most faculty members have an overriding sense of identity with their institution.There is a striving for a sense of community and a desire to be a part of the whole. Chart 2 indicates that across the nation chief academic officers perceive a solid sense of faculty identity with the curriculum and other instructional concerns. It is interesting to note that these tendencies of faculty ownership seem to be slightly higher at the larger institutions.

Developing a strong sense of support for teaching is not an easy task. It requires constant attention and action on numerous fronts.

## Chart 2
### Impact of Faculty Curriculum Ownership on
### Instructional Effectiveness by Size of Institution

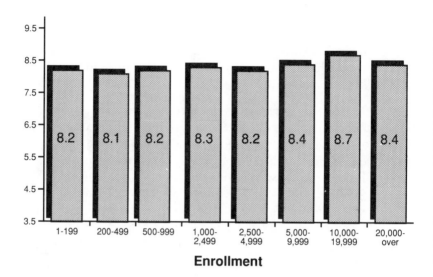

**Enrollment**

A vice president at a regional midwestern university expressed his dismay by noting that "efforts to improve teaching effectiveness through workshops, seminars, etc., have had very limited success because of poor faculty attendance.Those that do attend, need it least." The academic vice chancellor at a southern university characterized the complexity of this task by stating:

> As institutions drive toward enhanced reputations based on research productivity and extramural funding levels, their concern for imaginative advances in teaching and curriculum development may wane. We must guard against homogenization in our system of higher education, including the tendency for all to emulate the "research university."

> Our university is a doctorate-granting institution of moderate size, with a deep commitment to undergraduate education as well as to graduate study. Research is being emphasized more in recent years, as is appropriate given our mission. In this context, it is quite natural that some faculty lament, "the only thing that counts around here any more is research

53

and publications/exhibition." I do not advocate backing away from a newfound commitment or research. But, I do think this must be paralleled by renewed vigor toward instruction, lest we lose sight of the central purpose of our institution. The challenge is to find innovative means to support, expect and reward quality teaching as well as excellence in research, and to channel service activities out of these fundamental endeavors.

In an institution that is not a research university, but one necessarily concerned with research productivity, the faculty should be encouraged to conduct quality research all along the "innovation chain." Practice sensitive research should be as revered as fundamental research, if a distinction must be made, so long as it is first-rate. The closer research comes to practical problems in the professions or disciplines, the greater the likelihood such activity can draw students close to research activity and draw research findings to the classroom.

We have fostered increased attention and support for research. In parallel, I have tried, with less success, to encourage and support excellence in teaching. Unfortunately, teaching is often taken for granted and those concerned with institutional reputation often make the mistake, in my judgment, of letting research activity stand as the principle source of reputational advantage. I am happy to see more rhetoric about curriculum reform and teaching excellence come from foundations, national agencies, and research institutions. Perhaps some real advances may follow.

There is a lack of imagination manifested in ineffective teaching evaluation systems and unwillingness to offer grant programs for creative teaching/curriculum projects. I remain frustrated by the struggle to encourage administrative attention across the institution for instructional advancements. I am still limited to a relatively small allocation from indirect cost recovery funds to support the instructional improvement grant program (about $35,000 per year). Well over $200,000 is allocated for intra-mural research grants support.

## Ideas for Action

A strong sense of faculty ownership in the curricular process is entirely appropriate and probably deserves a higher rating. To achieve increased levels of faculty commitment to the instructional process, several steps should be taken:

- Develop policies and procedures that facilitate faculty involvement in the critical academic and institutional processes -- utilize academic planning as a primary institutional driving force, maintain integrity in the essential academic procedures, and solicit broad faculty input on institutional initiatives.

- Maintain a high level of faculty dialogue in internal governance structures -- provide opportunity for faculty-based structures to function, utilize existing structures whenever possible, and encourage faculty participation in instructional activities.

- Promote the application of high standards in peer and program reviews -- exhibit traits of fairness, consistency and rigor, demonstrate an openness to curricular change and innovation, and support initiatives that illustrate the importance of students and their education.

- Demonstrate an administrative leadership style that respects the principles of shared responsibility -- solicit input, listen/listen/listen, maintain flexibility, and make clear decisions.

- Stimulate initiatives that promote program, curricular, and instructional changes -- support curricular innovations, extend curriculum development activities, and promote outcomes assessment approaches.

- Encourage faculty to initiate program changes within disciplines and in general education -- study national reports from various disciplinary orientations, utilize outside peer reviews and consultants, and insist on clear statements of purpose, objectives, and evaluation.

• Incorporate course and curriculum development activities as a significant portion of the teaching assessment process -- review instructional materials in all personnel actions, balance in-class performance with class preparation activities, and assess effectiveness of departmental assessment procedures.

## Intellectual Vitality

Intellectual vitality is one of the most important characteristics of an outstanding teacher. As described in previous chapters, stressing the importance of teaching does not lessen the need for faculty members to be practicing scholars. Nor, does it suggest that research and creative endeavors are unimportant. To the contrary, teaching excellence demands disciplinary competence. If anything, the elevation of teaching suggests that there must be various means of assessing one's intellectual vitality. Traditional approaches that focus attention only on one's publishing record may, in fact, be one of the least effective approaches for making such judgments.

While one's intellectual activity affects classroom performance, faculty morale in general can influence the overall teaching environment. Poor morale can be a deterrent to productive scholarship; it can weaken the instructional process. It can contribute negatively to changes that otherwise might be perceived as being a positive accomplishment. Even placing more emphasis on teaching may be perceived by some as changing the rules, which may have a negative effect on their morale. In matters of this type, attention needs to be given to both the up- and down-side of the issue.

---

*If anything, the elevation of teaching suggests that there must be various means of assessing one's intellectual vitality. Traditional approaches that focus attention only on one's publishing record may, in fact, be one of the least effective approaches for making such judgments.*

---

Chart 3 suggests that the perceived degree to which intellectual vitality and morale contributes to instructional effectiveness is relatively modest. The impact is essentially constant, regardless of the size of the institution. The mean ratings in the mid-7 range suggest that efforts to enhance this area could greatly strengthen the level of instructional effectiveness on most campuses.

**Chart 3**
**Intellectual Vitality and Morale Contributions on**
**Instructional Effectiveness by Size of Institution**

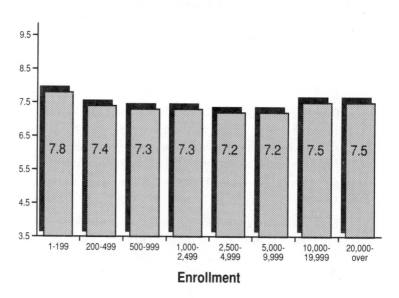

Again, the ratings represented in Chart 3 leave plenty of room for administrative leadership. The task is more than stressing the positive and effectively countering the negative. Many academic leaders have found that this is not as easy as it may seem. An academic leader at a California institution revealed part of the dilemma: "This university does not value academic endeavors. I work to support department chairs and faculty. The President berates the faculty personally and in groups. We have high turnover of faculty/staff." At a comparable eastern institution, the chief academic officer emphasized that "this is an institution in transition. It is directly addressing questions raised in this survey. We are now at the point often described as the intersection of the Missouri mule and the 2 x 4." At another southern university, the academic vice president pointed out that "negative factors influence the rate at which positive change occurs. My efforts are limited to reducing the negative forces."

## Ideas for Action

To make progress in the areas of intellectual vitality and morale, institutional leaders need to:

- •Set aside the singular approach of evaluating research and publications, and develop alternative means of demonstrating faculty intellectual vitality -- assess in-class performance, evaluate instructional materials, assess classroom scholarship, and critique curricular leadership abilities.

- •Create an action-oriented management team dedicated to dealing effectively with campus-wide concerns -- address volatile issues in a timely fashion, foster a positive working environment for all employees, and maintain an open intellectual environment.

- •Establish and maintain an open communication system that promotes a candid sharing of factual information -- develop open budgetary processes that encourage faculty participation, respond regularly to concerns based upon faulty or misinformation, and regularly share assessment information about the institution's programs.

- •Support those campus efforts that stimulate outstanding scholarship and classroom excellence - - promote instructionally based research and experimentation, recognize research and instructional excellence in all forms, regardless of how it might appear, and encourage those activities that promote both scholarship and teaching.

## Administrative Leadership

Administrative leadership is the single most important element that can shape the campus environment. It may take various forms and may be demonstrated by a variety of actions either on and off campus. The types of initiatives proposed by the upper administration, the manner in which decisions are made, the degree to which team actions are coordinated, and the overall style of leadership all contribute to the management style of the administration. When initiatives supporting teaching are added to the list of positive leadership qualities, the faculty are freed to devote greater attention to their professional responsibilities. The earlier reported national mean of 6.9 given by chief academic officers to their campus leadership does not speak well for the manner in which academic leaders are implementing these concepts. Chart 4 further illustrates that generally there is a drop in the perceived degree to which administrative leadership contributes to the overall effectiveness of the instructional program as one progresses toward larger institutions. Administrators should take notice that their influence on instructional effectiveness will probably decrease as the size of the institution increases. Added effort will likely be required to sustain high levels of leadership at larger institutions.

## Chart 4
## Impact of Administrative Leadership on
## Instructional Effectiveness by Size of Institution

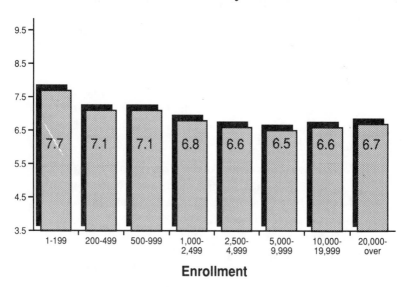

**Enrollment**

In the process of conducting the research, numerous examples were collected that demonstrated strong campus-wide leadership. Many of these items are used to make specific points in the chapters that follow. Two particularly noteworthy examples illustrate ways in which administrative leadership can elevate the importance of teaching. First, at Stanford University, the Center for Teaching and Learning has published an eighty-page monograph **Teaching and Stanford: An Introductory Handbook for Faculty, Academic Staff/Teaching, and Teaching Assistants**. In the foreward, President Donald Kennedy stressed the importance of effective teaching and stated:

> Teaching of such quality does not happen accidentally; like successful research, it requires hard thought, sufficient time, repeated effort, and the careful monitoring and evaluation of results. Above all, it demands personal engagement. Successful teachers are those for whom teaching changes with every class and every group of students. These are the teachers who continually refine their examples, go over lecture notes even when they are well-known, handle all questions with respect, and involve students in their work in formal and informal ways.

The handbook provides specific examples, "dos and don'ts", and helpful insights into the major topics of course preparation, getting started, common teaching situations, teaching and grading, evaluating and improving teaching, interaction with students, teaching and research, and teaching resources.

A second example that illustrates the importance of teaching was found in the long-range plan at the University of Idaho. In the introduction to their plan, the importance of teaching and curricular revision was emphasized:

> **Teaching.** The strength of the University's instructional program rests on the quality of its teaching. New faculty will be recruited with major attention to their potential to be outstanding teachers. Teaching improvement and faculty development programs will be established, and outstanding teaching will be recognized and rewarded in faculty evaluations and in considerations for promotion and tenure.

> **Curricular Revision.** The role and mission statement for the University recognizes major areas of responsibility to include agriculture, architecture, en-

gineering, forestry, wildlife and range sciences, law, and mining and metallurgy, as well as designated areas in the arts and sciences, business and education. The focus for these major programs during the next decade will be on curricular reform to address changing technological, social and public policy needs. Closer association with private sector clientele, emphasis on internships, practical and field experience, and incorporation of interdisciplinary course work will help produce professionally oriented, highly qualified graduates.

Of equal importance will be the commitment to produce graduates who are broadly educated, well-rounded adults with a continuing desire for new knowledge. To this end, the disciplines represented in the core curriculum will assume greater responsibility for strengthening the undergraduate curriculum and providing experiences for students to broaden their general knowledge, skills, and experiences.

The leadership response to this charge was a set of fifteen goals and management strategies. Goal IX states the intent of the University of Idaho to "Attract, Develop and Retain Quality Faculty". Twenty-one strategies were delineated to guide future actions:

### Attract

1. Achieve salary levels and benefit options comparable with those of peer institutions.

2. Provide adequate resources for faculty recruitment and relocation.

3. Provide summer, career-related job opportunities for productive new faculty.

4. Conduct an annual orientation program for new faculty and staff.

## Develop

5. Develop more explicit, institution-wide policies and procedures that recognize and reward excellence in teaching.

6. Provide training and orientation for administrators and department heads.

7. Institute an active faculty development program.

8. Improve the quality of instruction by integrating course evaluation and information with faculty development plans.

9. Establish an endowed fund for faculty development.

10. Increase the amount of travel funds available to faculty for professional development purposes.

11. Enhance the sabbatical leave program.

12. Develop faculty exchange programs.

13. Provide incentives for faculty to teach innovative courses.

14. Encourage the use of released time and flexible scheduling to assist faculty in developing and revising their courses and in their research, writing and creative endeavors.

## Retain

15. Improve non-monetary incentives and benefits.

16. Recognize and reward faculty who generate external funds.

17. Ensure faculty participation in University governance and decision-making.

18. Promote collegiality and positive self-image.

19. Provide training in areas of research methods, computers and statistics.

20. Provide equipment and services to support the faculty in their teaching, research and service activities.

21. Establish endowed chairs.

## Ideas for Action

The list of administrative leadership opportunities is long. To provide a more conducive learning atmosphere that stimulates effective instruction, academic and executive officers need to:

- Provide constant institutional leadership that addresses day-to-day concerns and maintains an orientation directed toward the future -- establish a mechanism to clearly articulate future plans, communicate institutional positions in a positive manner, and encourage activities that facilitate effective decision making.

- Support in an extraordinary manner those activities that enhance, expand, and extend the importance of teaching on campus -- issue position papers or statements that demonstrate institutional positions on teaching, reward (formally and informally) actions that promote effective instruction, and maintain high visibility for instructionally related activities.

- Build an administrative team with strong competencies in their specialty areas that understands the instructional mission of the institution -- manage by example, deal effectively with people, and address the service orientation of all employees.

- Establish academic and institutional planning processes that build a sense of institutional identity -- effectively involve various constituencies, regularly chart future directions, and routinely make decisions that implement the plans.

## Institutional Pride

There are a number of sources that can generate and contribute to a sense of institutional pride. Typically, academic quality is the primary force that supports a strong feeling of pride. High quality may be exhibited by the academic standards maintained by students, expectations held for promotion and tenure, level of teaching and scholarship, institutional accomplishments and academic successes, and recognition in support areas such as public service, community relations, and athletics. Close connections exist between institutional pride and teaching. A high sense of institutional pride can influence daily actions. If there is a strong sense of pride, faculty will likely expect more and give more in the classroom setting. They will regularly communicate positive images to students, who in turn feel better about the institution and promote its success. This cyclic tendency can be a major contributor to institutional pride and success. Chart 5 points out that strong efforts are needed to improve the overall sense of institutional pride on most campuses. Furthermore, the degree to which chief academic officers perceived institutional pride affecting instructional effectiveness declines substantially as the size of the institution increases. Again, this size differential places added burdens on the academic administrators in larger institutions.

### Chart 5
### Impact of Institutional Pride on
### Instructional Effectiveness by Size of Institution

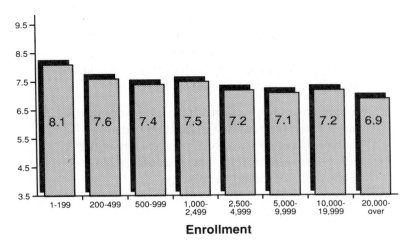

**Enrollment**

A high level of pride can be expressed in all institutional activities. It can be reflected in the professional attitudes and actions of all employees. Institutional pride is composed of all of the items already referred to (administrative stability, faculty ownership, intellectual vitality, and administrative leadership), along with a myriad of formal and informal actions. Even what may seem to be an inconsequential event in a department can influence a portion of the campus.

## Ideas for Action

The possibilities for administrative leadership, both direct and indirect, are immense. Areas in which strong leadership might strengthen the level of pride include activities designed to:

- Establish ongoing mechanisms (internally and externally) that positively promote the quality of the institution -- utilize measures of academic achievement (faculty and student), incorporate routine activities (program reviews, curricular improvements and personnel changes) into promotional efforts, and give high visibility to accreditation accomplishments, consultant reports, and other outside assessments.

- Develop a sense of faculty/staff ownership in the operation of the institution -- seek broad input into the decision making process, recognize individual contributions in institutional successes, and promote decision making at all levels of the institution.

- Provide positive working conditions for all employees that foster a sense of self worth and dignity -- meet with various employee groups whenever possible, be visible on campus and at events that are important to various segments of the campus, and maintain "employee sensitive" policies.

- Demonstrate institutional responsiveness to problems and issues that come before the campus -- assess the various perspectives of an issue, encourage decision making at the appropriate level, and address concerns in a forthright manner.

## Leadership Opportunity

The perceptions of chief academic officers across the nation clearly indicate that tremendous opportunities are present for all campuses to strengthen the context for teaching. Strong leadership initiatives can shape or create a more positive teaching/learning environment. Initiatives and plans of action need not be elaborate or detailed. They do, however, need to be focused on teaching and sustained over a long period of time. The examples and illustrations provided in this chapter suggest a framework that can sustain leadership in the areas of faculty ownership, institutional pride, and intellectual vitality. Administrative actions can be used to promote a strong teaching culture. Little can be achieved, however, in isolation; teaching must be made a campus-wide priority.

The growing body of literature in higher education suggests various alternatives for strong, creative leadership. Further insights may be gained from reading about broader topics such as situational management, corporate culture, the context for learning, and implementing change. Regardless of the sources of information or the alternatives pursued, it is clear that leadership must be forthcoming from the upper-level administrative officers. Haphazard efforts and unplanned initiatives will do little more than compound the existing situation and frustrate efforts to strengthen teaching on most college campuses.

---

*Strong leadership initiatives can shape or create a more positive teaching/learning environment. Initiatives and plans of action need not be elaborate or detailed ... Little can be achieved, however, in isolation; teaching must be made a campus-wide priority.*

---

# Chapter Six

## EMPLOYMENT POLICIES AND PRACTICES

On most campuses, employment-related activities command a great deal of attention. For the larger campus it can typically involve literally hundreds of individuals, while on smaller campuses one or two persons often carry the entire burden. The breadth, diversity, and complexity of the practices used in the nation's colleges and universities are beyond simple description. Not only does each institution have its own policies and procedures, but each has distinctive features built around unique qualities and characteristics. It is not surprising to find, therefore, that chief academic officers rank employment policies and practices as the strongest category used to demonstrate institutional commitment to instructional effectiveness.

Regardless of campus size, the typical academic administrator is besieged with employment-related issues and problems. As a work priority, personnel items require enormous time commitments and drains vast amounts of energy. The sources of these demands are varied and tend to compound the complexity of the area. The administrator must have broad knowledge of the network of campus policies and procedures to ensure a consistent application of guiding principles. Campus governance committees often devote most of their attention to employment-related issues. The nationwide trend toward greater "legalism" has increased the demands for greater specificity and precision. Finally, of course, individual meetings and conferences with faculty members consume great amounts of time and energy. While anxieties and frustrations often "run high" in these settings, each experience provides administrators with an added opportunity to stress the importance of teaching. Actions taken in support of teaching excellence may be expressed in a variety of ways, such as taking a strong position in a campus debate, through the issuance of a written statement, or on an informal basis in a personal conference.

It is important, too, for administrators to understand the context in which issues are raised. In some cases, the best that can be achieved is a demonstration of being sensitive to the faculty perspective. For example, the natural expectation of all faculty members is that they will receive tenure or promotion. While this is a most desirous trait, negative action can only be perceived as a failure of the system. Since teaching evaluative systems are notoriously weak, the blame is commonly placed on other areas. Thus, it may be common to hear that "teaching is not as important around here as is publishing." To make matters more difficult, notes a dean of instruction at a small western institution, it is common on many campuses to assume that everyone is a good teacher:

> Much of my dissatisfaction is the result of an institutional climate that **assumes** good teaching is taking place, but gives little attention to teaching, **per se**. I believe much of the instruction here is excellent, but the assumption that we need not work on it, evaluate courses regularly, etc., is unproductive. We are about to discuss yet again the question of requiring course evaluations -- perhaps I'll be more optimistic after that's over, depending on the quality of the discussion primarily, and only secondarily the outcome.

An academic vice president at an eastern regional campus expressed his frustration with the institution's unwillingness to improve the level of commitment to teaching.

> I remain surprised that a campus which prides itself on good teaching has done so little over the decades to promulgate it. Let me clarify. First, our faculty are fine and dedicated teachers. They work hard at their craft and are, by all accounts, successful. Second, it is odd, however, that we have few means by which to measure our accomplishments in the teaching arena. In fact, it continues to be a source of frustration for our Promotion and Tenure Committee and me. Third, when I recently polled the faculty about their faculty development interests, I was surprised to learn they had little enthusiasm for focusing faculty development on teaching improvement. Fourth, the issue of validating effective teaching is an important issue to all comprehensive universities particularly in light of the national mania for program assessment.

In a similar vein, the dean of instruction at a small private institution in California noted that:

> Teaching excellence is the highest criterion for hiring, tenure, etc. The campus climate, faculty, and staff support and promote its primacy. However, I think we need to do much more in terms of faculty development -- there's a little bit of the 'we're all terrific teachers already' ethic that makes me move cautiously in this area.

A counterpart across the nation reported some successes in this area:

> Some faculty have made serious efforts to develop a learner-centered focus. Teaching skill is our highest evaluative criterion for faculty. Since we are a small institution, our primary focus is on monitoring and nurturing effective teaching skills for relatively small classroom situations.

The complexity of the employment category is also illustrated by the degree to which it is connected with other aspects of the campus. The legitimacy of the evaluation and reward systems, for example, can be affected by faculty discontentment over governance issues. Morale will most likely be weakened if there is not a sense of ownership, participation, or consultation in the deliberative process. Similarly, if the role of the part-time faculty is not clear, conflicts may arise. Fundamental to these issues, the provost at a major southern research institution pointed out that there must be a balance in the reward system:

> We have considerable difficulty emphasizing teaching on an equal basis with research. Where we do succeed, it's when teaching is not a secondary function but equal to research. There are fully faculty members with both talents. We want them.

The complexity of the challenge to strengthen the commitment to teaching in all aspects of employment requires multiple actions. While a single initiative might be used to illustrate a point, sustained efforts are needed in faculty selection, promotion, development, evaluation, and recognition. Consideration must be given to the wholeness of the employment process and the impact on individual decisions, behavior, and attitudes.

## Supportive Nature of Employment Policies
## and Practices

The formal and informal employment policies and practices of an institution and the behavior of administrators and faculty members dictate, in a large measure, the overall level of commitment to teaching. Some may question the motivation behind an action or the intent of a policy, but the actual employment decisions influence much of what is said and done about teaching on campus. While administrators devote a large portion of their time and energy to personnel items, care must be taken that whenever possible special attention is given to teaching. Theoretically, an administrator could say that all of his or her time is devoted to improving instructional effectiveness. While this may be true, in reality much of the time is devoted to human relations. These differences in perception may explain why administrators sense a strong commitment to the use of employment practices to enhance teaching effectiveness, while at the same time, faculty members typically cite this area as the one that requires the greatest level of improvement on the part of administrators. Regardless of the situation, the opportunity for improvement is substantial. The challenge to academic leaders is to extend the ways in which outstanding teaching is emphasized, evaluated on a periodic basis, used as a major criterion for promotion, rewarded in a substantial fashion, and promoted on an institutional basis.

---

*While administrators devote a large portion of their time and energy to personnel items, care must be taken that whenever possible special attention is given to teaching.*

---

Table 9 presents an overall perspective of the views of the chief academic officers on using employment policies and practices to support instructional effectiveness. Not only did this category receive the highest rating by academic leaders, it also had the three highest ranked items: evaluating teaching by students, evaluating teaching for tenure, and evaluating teaching for promotion. Only 70 percent of the chief academic officers rated the use of teaching evidence in the hiring process at the good/excellent level. About half of the officers rated teaching recognition programs at this level. While these practices received favorable ratings, when combined with the item on recognition and rewards, they represent some of the most controversial elements in the dialogue about effective teaching. Faculty evaluation questionnaires typically generate two basic questions on most campuses: First, to what extent will teaching effectiveness data be used in making personnel decisions? Second, how effective are the instruments, procedures, and processes used in measuring teaching excellence? In most cases, the answer to both questions is that teaching is an important factor, but significant improvement is needed. Improvements in faculty assessment and evaluation must be the leading force in the reform movement if a new emphasis on teaching is to be implemented successfully.

## Table 9
### Perceived Commitment of Employment Policies and Practices in Support of Instructional Effectiveness

| Items | % Rating 1, 2, or 3 | Mean | % Rating 8, 9, or 10 |
|---|---|---|---|
| Classroom instruction is regularly evaluated by students | 2 | 9.1 | 88 |
| Teaching effectiveness is evaluated as a significant/integral aspect of the tenure process | 1 | 9.1 | 88 |
| Teaching effectiveness is evaluated as a significant/integral aspect of the promotion process | 2 | 8.9 | 86 |
| A faculty member's teaching effectiveness is evaluated as a significant/integral aspect of the initial hiring process | 4 | 8.0 | 70 |
| Teaching recognition programs (grants, awards, etc.) that promote effective teaching are available | 14 | 7.0 | 51 |

*Faculty evaluation questionnaires typically generate two basic questions on most campuses: First, to what extent will teaching effectiveness data be used in making personnel decisions? Second, how effective are the instruments, procedures, and processes used in measuring teaching excellence?*

While secondary to the evaluation agenda, the level of attention given to faculty selection and hiring practices and to recognition and reward activities must be dramatically increased. The assessment of teaching competencies has lagged behind other evaluative efforts in most faculty selection processes. Several institutions are beginning more systematically to review teaching data and instructional materials for full-time faculty members. Important strides have also been made in improving the preparation of graduate teaching assistants. Few institutions devote much attention to the teaching skills of their part-timers, who may offer as much as twenty to thirty percent of the instruction. The issue of rewards and recognition has become increasingly important to some faculty members. It, too, is a "double-edged sword." Greater recognition often results in merit programs that are often resented by a large portion of the faculty. Significant changes in campus reward systems will occur only when substantial improvements are made in the evaluation process. While this is a "tender point" with many faculty members, the accountability forces will continue to push the profession toward increased levels of assessment and evaluation.

---

*Significant changes in campus reward systems will occur only when substantial improvements are made in the evaluation process.*

---

## Faculty Selection

Teaching competency and the assessment of these skills have been relatively weak links in the faculty selection process. In recent years, it has become more common to require prospective faculty members to conduct a teaching session on campus, present video tapes of past performances, provide student evaluation data, and submit examples of instructional materials and curricular activities. The general practices in these areas, however, leave much to be desired. Similarly, the teaching credentials of part-time faculty members are seldom thoroughly reviewed. Chart 6 indicates that the extent of this problem is substantially greater at larger institutions. The chief academic officers reported a progressively higher rating up to an institutional enrollment of about 2500. At this point, the assessment of teaching in the selection process declines in a similar fashion. The 6.6 mean rating for the largest institutions suggests an extremely low commitment to the review of teaching credentials in the initial employment process.

In reflecting on the importance of the faculty selection process, the Dean of Faculty at Harvey Mudd College in California emphasized that:

I have been dean of faculty for fourteen years. During that time I have noticed that our truly outstanding teachers were excellent right from the start of their careers. Thus, we work very hard to identify outstanding teaching ability when we invite a candidate for a faculty position to the campus. I also make it clear that, while we expect every faculty member to engage in scholarly activity, we are an undergraduate teaching college, not a research university. Our priority, both for reappointments and salary increases, is excellence in teaching. Young faculty members are expected to develop a research program, but that is primarily to provide undergraduate research opportunities for students and to make certain that faculty members stay current in their areas of specialty.

## Chart 6
## Impact of Teaching Evaluations in the Hiring Process on Instructional Effectiveness by Size of Institution

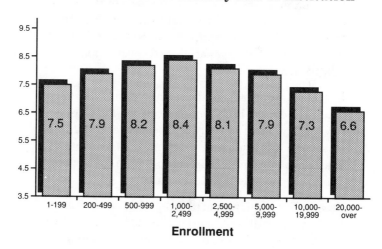

At Shorter College in Georgia, the Vice President for Academic Affairs and Dean of the College reported:

Every candidate for a teaching position at Shorter College must present a teaching demonstration as part of the interviewing process. The subject of the demonstration must be something that is included in our curriculum and not a presentation of the dissertation. The candidate may choose the style. The length of the demonstration is confined to the normal class length. All faculty and students are invited to attend. A rating sheet is usually distributed. The division chairman considers the ratings and any other comments given by those in attendance before a recommendation is made to the Vice President for Academic Affairs and Dean of the College.

Describing a more comprehensive approach at Troy State University in Montgomery, Alabama, the Vice President for Academic Affairs pointed out the importance of initial teaching demonstrations and ongoing evaluation.

We employ a large cadre of professionals from the community as adjunct faculty, because we believe that these teachers who bring practical experience to the classroom enhance the learning experience. These professionals often are not academicians, however, and may need to be nurtured in the development of sound instructional practices. Full-time faculty, on the other hand, often need to be refreshed and reminded of innovative methods to motivate adult learners.

For these and other sound reasons, several years ago we initiated teaching demonstrations for prospective faculty whom we had not observed teaching, and classroom visitation and observation at least once a year by the program coordinator, dean and/or academic vice president for all faculty.

Prospective faculty seem to accept the teaching demonstration readily. It is accomplished in one of two ways. He/she may prepare to teach a segment of an ongoing class as a guest instructor, after which the students are asked to submit their reactions to the dean. Appropriate academic administrators are usually present. If no appropriate class is available, a group of faculty, staff, and volunteer students will be convened to serve as a "class" to which the prospective instructor is given a chance to prepare and present a typical lesson. The "class" is then asked to provide written reactions to the dean.

## Ideas for Action

These examples vividly illustrate the importance of considering teaching effectiveness in the faculty selection process and that successful efforts are underway to improve this function. Teaching effectiveness can be enhanced through the refinement of faculty selection procedures by:

- Evaluating effectively classroom teaching competence during the pre-employment process -- establish ongoing procedures to assess classroom competencies in a campus presentation during the employment interview, review student evaluations from other institutions, and analyze video tapes and other materials that characterize one's teaching style.

- Promoting the significance of teaching throughout the faculty recruitment process -- state the importance of teaching in position descriptions and advertisements, articulate in the interview the role of teaching on campus in terms of promotion, tenure, merit awards, etc., and ensure that the importance of teaching is clearly referred to in descriptive materials about the institution.

- Assessing the full range of teaching in the selection process -- assess the candidate's disciplinary competence, measure his or her instructional and curriculum development leadership skills, and evaluate organizational plans and instructional materials used in teaching.

- Insisting on the demonstration of teaching competence in the employment of all candidates who have recently completed doctoral programs -- review evidence of teaching knowledge and competence as demonstrated in the doctoral program, require yearlong seminars on teaching for full-time individuals entering the college teaching profession, and stress the interrelatedness between scholarship and effective instruction.

- Establishing standard teaching assessment mechanisms for all part-time teaching faculty members -- develop short-term (pre-employment and ongoing) seminars and workshops focused on specific teaching techniques; provide instructional guides, outlines, and materials that facilitate effective instruction; and integrate the evaluation of instruction offered by part-time employees into the regular assessment procedures.

## Periodic Review

The periodic review of instruction provided by faculty members is one of the most important ingredients in the formula to ensure effective instruction. It provides an ongoing means to judge intellectual vitality and teaching competence. It serves as a means to measure student learning and assess outcomes. It provides a data base for performance appraisal, self-analysis, and improvement. It serves as a primary medium for the institution to demonstrate its commitment to instructional effectiveness.

The care with which the evaluation system is developed significantly contributes to its overall effectiveness. The approaches utilized to evaluate instruction must be perceived as equitable by those affected by its use. The evaluation forms must demonstrate the importance of teaching. At Sam Houston State University, for example, the form itself is weighted to demonstrate clearly the importance of teaching:

> The "Teaching" factor must be weighted higher than any of the other factors. Each year, the individual faculty member may select the weights to be assigned to the factors to be used in his/her evaluation, but the weights for the factors must be within the ranges indicated for each factor. Teaching must be weighted from 40 percent to 60 percent; Scholastic and Artistic Endeavor from 10 percent to 30 percent; Professional Growth and Activities from 5 percent to 20 percent; and Non-Teaching Activities Supportive of University Programs from 10 percent to 25 percent. The total weights chosen must, of course, total 100 percent. The teaching factor must be weighted more than any other factor, which reinforces our

university's premise that we expect more than just teaching from faculty members, but teaching is, indeed, the most important aspect of their total performance.

Instructional improvement strategies (expanded upon in Chapters 7 and 9) must incorporate diagnostic and consultative aspects not normally found in systems that evaluate professional competence for a personnel action. The basic differences in goals of the approaches designed for self-improvement and evaluation emphasize the need for the separateness. Policies must carefully distinguish between evaluative judgments aimed at promotion, tenure, merit, and salary considerations and those activities directed toward self-improvement. Regardless of the purpose, however, a variety of sources of information should be used to document the full range of teaching effectiveness, including organization, preparation, and performance. Whenever possible, normative data should be collected that compares faculty who teach in reasonably similar situations. The evaluation should include all faculty members (tenured, untenured, and part-time) responsible for providing instruction.

Chart 7 indicates that student evaluations contribute to the periodic review process in a consistently high manner throughout the

**Chart 7**
**Impact of Student Evaluations on**
**Instructional Effectiveness by Size of Institution**

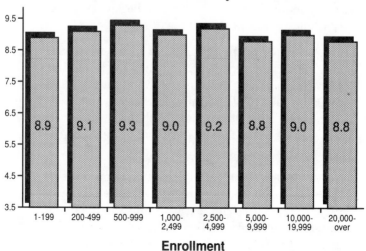

**Enrollment**

academic community. The use of student input in the evaluation process was rated as the highest ranked item in the twenty-five statements. Narrative comments collected as a part of the research, however, indicated that chief academic officers were not nearly as positive about the ongoing nature of the peer review process. The academic vice president at a college in the southwest noted that the process to develop peer reviews can be slow and tedious:

> In the past few years, changes in governance have given to department chairs a heightened responsibility in the evaluation and review of their colleagues. Even before this official responsibility, we are trying to encourage a climate in which all faculty visit each other's classes, share observations and work collaboratively on improving their effectiveness as teachers. In this transition period, we still have strong reservations on the part of some individuals to assess such activity, and a likelihood many department chairs will never have observed directly a colleague in the classroom or have discussed specifically some reported or perceived weakness. I believe all faculty can improve and can respond more positively to constructive criticism from colleagues rather than from an administrator whose evaluations are at once both more removed and more threatening. One hurdle to surmount is to get colleagues to be honest with each other and not to avoid evaluation or to mislead.

A vice president at a major eastern university stressed that political situations often slow the process.

> A number of the department heads were once peers of faculty members, and they work and live with them on a daily basis. Quite often they and their families relate socially. Because of that, it is sometimes difficult for some of them to relate the weaknesses to the faculty members in their department.

> To the few "political" departments, it is difficult for department heads to relate weaknesses of faculty members to them, because that can create an upsetting political situation in the department. This can be exacerbated because occasionally weak

faculty are able to attract the support of peers and thus the dissension in the department spreads.

Despite these aforementioned observations, I would also like to relate that over time our department heads have become more and more comfortable and more and more proficient in implementing a merit pay system and in providing objective but humane evaluations of our faculty. Thus, over time, the implementation of explicit and objective evaluations are becoming more successful.

At Troy State University in Montgomery, the Vice President for Academic Affairs has tried to balance the need for evaluation with sensitivity and positive feedback:

When the faculty was informed that each instructor would be visited at least once each year by an academic administrator, there was some expression of violation of academic freedom by some few faculty. A few adjunct faculty declined to continue teaching. The Council of Deans and I wrestled at length with the structure for these classroom visits and finally gave up on a University-wide plan for structuring the observation and feedback and left that up to each dean. The results have been gratifying. Faculty have accepted the visits as helpful. Usually the dean or program coordinator does not announce his visit but does take steps to learn that a typical class session will take place on that evening. Some deans participate in discussions of the class, others sit quietly in the back of the classroom and observe. All provide written feedback to the instructor; sometimes just an acknowledgement of the visit with no evaluation, and other times with recommendations for improvement or comments on positive aspects of the class.

One aspect of our commitment to excellence in teaching, on which I did not comment earlier, may need mentioning. When summaries of the student course evaluations reach my office each quarter, I review them and write to each instructor who has been perceived by his students as being superior. I believe that faculty who do an exceptionally good job need recognition regularly. We administrators tend to expect excellence and then not recognize it, except at milestones like promotion and tenure time, but we are quick to criticize inferior performance. It has been my philosophy that superior performance in teaching requires the same nurturing as less adequate performance.

The comprehensive nature of evaluation was illustrated by the chief academic officer at Utah State University when he reported that a major strategic planning effort was underway.

Undergraduate learning is under intensive study by a University task force which is part of a Faculty Senate committee. This committee will write the component of the University's Strategic Plan which deals with undergraduate affairs. Among other tasks, it will address the question of the evaluation and rewards for instruction as opposed to research and service. In this latter regard, our biggest problem is one of administrative credibility. Teaching evaluations, such as they are, are taken fully into account by the central administration when it reviews promotion and tenure applications; the faculty, however, are not convinced this is the case. Also, as is true throughout this nation, the tools of evaluation of teaching and the means to help faculty improve their teaching are not precise or well established. These matters will be addressed in the Strategic Plan.

## Ideas for Action

The need to establish the periodic review of all instruction as one of the major cornerstones of a strong commitment to instructional effectiveness is obvious. Like so many other areas, initiatives are needed on a variety of fronts to change attitudes and procedures affecting the evaluation of instruction. Efforts should be taken to:

• Develop an ongoing evaluative system for all faculty members that effectively integrates in-class evaluations -- collect and share student evaluation data with appropriate decision makers on a regular and systematic basis, conduct peer in-class evaluations on a semester basis, and complete department chairperson in-class evaluations on an annual basis.

• Institute comprehensive evaluation systems for all individuals involved in the instructional process -- evaluate on a regular basis all full-time faculty members regardless of rank or tenure status, review all instruction provided by part-time employees, and assess on a regular basis instruction provided by graduate teaching assistants.

• Establish a regular campus-wide teaching evaluation data system -- collect common data from all instructional units for comparative and analytical purposes, use separate portions of the system to support self-improvement and personnel evaluation, and individualize a portion of the system to accommodate methodological, content, and other differences in instructional modes.

• Expand the evaluative process of instruction to include the full range of aspects that contribute to effective instruction -- assess course development activities and instructional materials, measure in-class instructional performance and the demonstration of content expertise, and assess student learning outcomes.

• Establish formal means to educate faculty members about the faculty evaluation -- conduct workshops on how to construct and use evaluative instruments, establish structures that facilitate the improvement of various approaches to instructional evaluation, and provide current research findings on instructional evaluation.

## Tenure Evaluation

The success of any tenure evaluation process is highly dependent upon the original conditions spelled out for the new faculty member and the actions that transpire during the tenure review cycle. The amount of attention given to teaching in the recruitment process, how teaching is conveyed in initial contacts (in written form or casual conversation), and what statements are actually made in the tenure policy have a great deal to do with the manner in which teaching evaluations are perceived and handled. If little attention is given to teaching in the selection process or during initial contacts with colleagues, the message soon becomes clear -- "do what you need to do to be acceptable in the classroom and devote most of your time to what is really important." The actual written statements in the tenure policy are vitally important to providing an operational framework for teaching. The procedures, too, convey a sense of rigor and commitment to the basic processes inherent in effective teaching.

While contractual understandings, tenure policies, and colleague perceptions provide a context for the teaching environment, the actions taken during the tenure review cycle provide the "proof of the pudding". The real test is with the application of standards, the thoroughness of the periodic reviews, and the visible actions taken regarding one's progress toward tenure. Tenure must be an explicit decision, and the prominence of teaching must be made evident at every critical opportunity. Chart 8 indicates that chief academic officers across the nation perceive a strong commitment to teaching in the tenure review process. Along with student evaluation of instruction, this item had the highest ranking in the national survey. It is interesting to note, however, that the perceived commitment to teaching in the tenure process is considerably lower at those institutions with an enrollment under 200 and those over 20,000.

Most faculty members agree that the rigor and expectations associated with tenure have significantly increased in the last decade or two. In the past, some faculty members were awarded tenure without any review. Today, tenure usually requires a long, detailed assessment. There is a strong likelihood that these increased demands will continue to create stress among the faculty. Yet, in some cases, the magnitude of a tenure decision is overlooked, and colleagues continue to rely primarily on personal relationships. The profession can no longer tolerate such a lax attitude. Consideration must be given to the impact of a faculty member on student lives for the next three or four decades. Or, what about the million dollar plus investment in an individual by an institution when a tenure decision is made? Clearly, the tenure evaluation process **requires** the utmost care and attention to the teaching component. It **mandates** a comprehensive review process. It **demands** the highest of academic

## Chart 8
## Impact of Tenure Teaching Evaluations on
## Instructional Effectiveness by Size of Institution

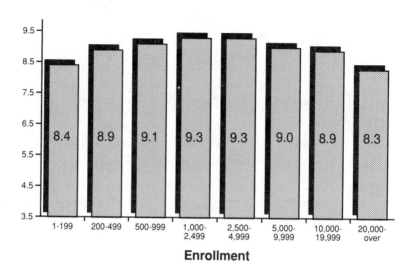

**Enrollment**

---

*Clearly, the tenure evaluation process requires the utmost care and attention to the teaching component. It mandates a comprehensive review process. It demands the highest of academic standards. It commands a natural blending of the scholarship/teaching responsibilities for deserving faculty members.*

---

standards. It **commands** a natural blending of the scholarship/ teaching responsibilities for deserving faculty members.

Each institution must substantially address these issues and move forward with their implementation. The procedures need not be complex, but their application must be rigorous. For example, the comprehensive review process at Rocky Mountain College could be summarized as follows:

> The Faculty Handbook requires that all tenure-track faculty be given a comprehensive evaluation during the second and sixth years of service, or in the year in which a tenured decision is to be made; and that tenure faculty be comprehensively reviewed every four years.

The comprehensive review consists of the following:

1.  Two meetings with the Dean, the first to be held at the beginning of the academic year for the purpose of goal setting, the second to be held at the end of the year for the purpose of evaluating the progress toward the goals set earlier. Faculty members are to prepare a written statement of goals and procedures to accomplish them, and bring it to the first meeting.

2.  Student evaluation of classes. You will be sent evaluation forms for students in all of your classes to complete and return to this office.

3.  Peer evaluations. Several faculty members, selected by you, should submit an evaluation to the Dean before the end of the spring semester. The deadline for this statement, and for those described below, will be stated later.

4.  Alumni evaluations. You are encouraged to solicit statements from alumni concerning your teaching. Such statements should be sent directly to the Dean.

5.  Advisee evaluations. A form will be sent to you before the beginning of spring term for you to distribute to your advisees. The form is to be returned directly to the Dean.

6.  Self-evaluation. The self-evaluation will be submitted at the time of the second conference with the Dean, in the spring (see 1 above).

## Ideas for Action

The critical nature of teaching in the tenure evaluation process emphasizes the need for most institutions to review existing tenure policies and the manner in which these procedures are utilized. Action should be taken to ensure the prominent role of teaching by:

• Analyzing the actual and perceived role of teaching in the tenure evaluation process -- review the actual language in the existing policy to ensure that teaching effectiveness receives proper attention, assess the application of teaching components in the tenure process to ensure consistency with the desired goals, and meet with academic leaders across the campus to gain further insights into the perceptions about teaching held by faculty members.

• Ensuring that tenure is an explicit process that measures specifically delineated teaching expectations and outcomes -- insist on a thorough application of the prescribed procedures, base decisions about teaching on data and information collected from a variety of sources, and use evaluations collected throughout the tenure review cycle to make judgments about teaching effectiveness.

• Requiring that teaching evaluations be based on the full range of teaching responsibilities -- evaluate in-class teaching performance and subject matter competence; review supportive teaching responsibilities, such as advising students, developing course and instructional materials, etc.; and assess the level of class preparation and organization.

• Initiating a thorough review of existing tenure policies in anticipation of the elimination of the seventy-year-old mandatory retirement law -- explore various alternatives available to ensure the maintenance of effective instruction, establish regular teaching review cycles (3-5 years) for all faculty members, and develop teaching performance objectives for all faculty members.

## Promotion Review

Like tenure evaluations, the promotion review process is highly dependent upon formal and informal statements of policy and the perceived nature of how these statements are implemented. Promotion, however, builds upon periodic tenure evaluations by asking faculty members to demonstrate more than their potential; it suggests that candidates are expected to rise above the normal level of performance. With respect to teaching, promotion means that a faculty member is better than the norm, has demonstrated teaching success with students, has evaluative support from colleagues, has implemented instructional and curricular improvements, and has demonstrated subject matter competence. As one progresses through the ranks, promotion demands an increased level of teaching proficiency. It reflects an increased integration of one's scholarship and teaching expertise. It assumes a broader application of one's subject matter and teaching competence.

Chief academic officers perceive teaching as an integral part of the promotion process in a manner similar to how they perceive tenure. Chart 9 reveals that in respect to promotion, those institutions with enrollments less than 500 and those over 20,000 fall into a group with lower levels of support for teaching. Again, the academic leaders from the institutions in the middle ranges demonstrate the strongest support for teaching.

**Chart 9**
**Impact of Promotion Teaching Evaluations on**
**Instructional Effectiveness by Size of Institution**

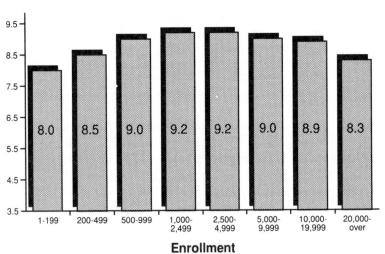

The relatively strong indications that administrators see teaching as a vital component in the promotion process, as well as with tenure, emphasize that the burden of responsibility to ensure a high level of commitment to teaching is a shared obligation. Faculty members cannot "pass the buck" to the administration. If any faculty member is promoted (or tenured) without evidence of strong teaching effectiveness, the primary responsibility for the substandard action rests with the faculty in the department. Administrators in the study demonstrated a strong commitment to teaching excellence. Faculty colleagues must accept the obligation to evaluate teaching if it is to be elevated to its rightful place.

As suggested earlier, there is a primary need for clear statements of expectation in the promotion policy. An approach used at Western Maryland College is to articulate some basic qualities of effective teaching.

> Effective teaching is a requisite for all faculty members at Western Maryland College. The College considers the following to be some of the verifiable signs of effective teaching:
>
> - Command of one's subject;
>
> - Knowledge of current developments in one's field;
>
> - Ability to relate one's subject to other areas of knowledge and endeavor;
>
> - Ability to provoke and broaden student interest in one's subject matter;
>
> - Ability to use effective and varied teaching methods and strategies;
>
> - Possession of discipline, integrity, industry, open-mindedness, and objectivity in teaching;
>
> - Recognition and knowledge of the general and individual needs of one's students;
>
> - Participation in special courses, seminars, or workshops which develop teaching skills;
>
> - Development or redesign of courses and curricula;
>
> - The ability to speak and write efficiently and effectively.

Specific language in evaluation materials can also be used to guide faculty members. At Southeast Missouri State University, the faculty and administration have jointly adopted departmentally based criteria. Each department has specifically stated criteria and performance levels to be achieved. This process is guided by university-wide suggestions on how to present evidence in the areas of teaching effectiveness, professional growth, and service. The section on teaching in the **Faculty Handbook** notes:

### Evidence of Teaching Effectiveness

None of the criteria is more important in the promotion process than that of teaching effectiveness. The faculty member, recognizing the inevitable range of opinion with respect to teaching effectiveness, should include all evidence accumulated as part of the promotional material. Submission of partial data from student ratings, for example, may be more detrimental than helpful. The complexity of this area suggests the collection of data from a variety of sources:

1. Course planning activities play an important role in subsequent classroom activities; for example, syllabi and course outlines, bibliographies, methods for testing and evaluation, texts, and assignments required of students may be used to demonstrate the quality of the planning process as it relates to teaching. Such insights may suggest the degree of sophistication in the entire learning process.

2. Classroom and laboratory activities form another measure of teaching effectiveness; for example, student and peer evaluations of actual performance, peer evaluation of effectiveness of educational approaches, and the quality of faculty-student interaction are areas in which documentation could be provided. This information may be collected from observations by students, peers, and department chairpersons. (Instruments used and sampling or population information may also be helpful.)

3. Analyses of team-teaching situations, videotaped presentations, or group interactions may also be helpful.

4. Academic performance of students is another factor which may be considered in making judgments concerning teaching effectiveness. This might include such factors as appraisal of student development, evidence of students' ability to perform in subsequent sequence courses, demonstrable competencies, special student awards or recognition, placement and follow-up studies, creative exhibits and concerts developed by students.

5. Flexibility demonstrated in the teaching/learning process may also be used to substantiate the recommendation. In this respect, a faculty member may call attention to the extent of course revisions made, how objectives were met, and/or personal assessment mechanisms developed.

6. Other systematic reviews of instructional strategies appropriate to particular disciplines may also be helpful in adjudicating teaching effectiveness.

## Ideas for Action

The level at which teaching becomes an integral part of the promotion process obviously varies by institution. As the level of commitment is assessed, consideration should be given to:

• Establishing threshold levels of teaching excellence that exceed the "departmental average" -- based on promotion decisions on documented teaching evidence that exceeds the norm, collect evidence of teaching excellence from a variety of sources, including students, colleagues, alumni and administrators, and establish campus-wide levels and measures of acceptable teaching excellence.

• Developing clear statements and procedures that delineate the role of teaching in the promotion process -- adopt statements of instructional expectations for campus-wide use, prepare guides to assist faculty members in the effective preparation and documentation of teaching credentials, and state criteria levels for judging teaching performance.

- Integrating scholarship and subject matter expertise into the teaching assessment process -- make clear statements regarding the interrelatedness of teaching and scholarship and the purpose of scholarly activity, evaluate the infusion of one's scholarship into the assessment of instructional competence, and promote the use of research to enhance the instructional process.

- Requiring high levels of teaching competence before consideration is given to scholarship and other promotion criterion areas -- assess statements on teaching in existing policies to ensure their consistency with stated purposes, develop data collection procedures and evaluative approaches to a level commensurate with the importance of teaching, and review on a regular basis the actual application of the criteria in the decision-making process.

## Teaching Recognition

The call from faculty members across the nation is for greater recognition and reward for teaching excellence. Without question, there is a need to improve dramatically the recognition of teaching and systems of rewarding excellence in the classroom. Efforts that effectively integrate curricular development activities into the recognition process need to be strengthened. Reward structures that support the development of new instructional materials need to be created. Measures of classroom excellence need to be developed and refined to provide more precision. Data collection processes and evidence supporting outstanding teaching need to be implemented. Decision-making processes, particularly those involving peer assessment, need to be substantially upgraded. Direct connections need to be made between effective teaching, the means of self-improvement, and other forms of recognition. **Incentives for Faculty Vitality** edited by Roger G. Baldwin (1), suggests ways to accomplish some of these ideals and some of the pitfalls associated with making changes in these areas.

The entire approach to academic recognition needs to be systematically made comparable to the well-established reward structures for publication, research, and grant activities. As Richard Bortz (30: 169-170) pointed out in a recent chapter, faculty recognition programs need "to assist faculty members in planning, organizing, and documenting their professional activities and establish a basis for recognizing and rewarding faculty accomplishment."

The goals of the faculty recognition system are to:

- Assist faculty members in attaining their professional and career goals;

- Assist academic departments in attaining their organizational goals and continue providing leadership and service to their clientele;

- Foster cooperation in the department by using an approach that benefits individual faculty members and the department alike;

- Establish a system for documenting and reporting faculty activities;

- Articulate salary increases, merit pay, tenure and promotion in recognizing faculty accomplishment; and

- Provide a fair and equitable means of evaluating the activities and contributions of individual faculty members.

Teaching must remain foremost in such efforts. There are various external forces that set in motion professional and institutional rewards for research and publication. Teaching excellence requires a new set of structures that promote the teaching scholar concept. These structures must be built upon faculty/administrative evaluation models, data collection procedures and reward systems that extend far beyond the current level of teaching award tokenism. Chart 10 vividly illustrates the embarrassing level of support for teaching recognition and rewards on the nation's campuses. It suggests, too, one of the most dramatic trends in the survey. While the perceived level of commitment increases with the size of the institution, the needs are great across the board. In fact, the sheer size of some of the larger institutions may make the task more difficult than would be the case at a smaller institution.

## Chart 10
## Impact of Teaching Recognition on
## Institutional Effectiveness by Size of Institution

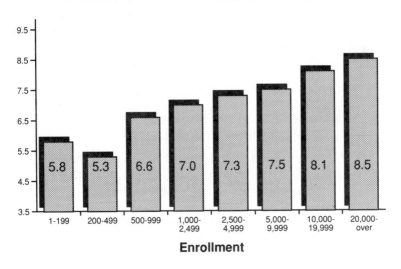

**Enrollment**

---

*Teaching excellence requires a new set of structures that promote the teaching scholar concept. These structures must be built upon faculty/administrative evaluation models, data collection procedures, and reward systems that extend far beyond current levels of teaching award tokenism .*

---

While the challenges are great, there are indications that significant changes are under way. The following illustrate a few such efforts that have been implemented. At Utah State University, for example, cash prizes are awarded annually for the Teacher of the Year by each College and by the University. The University winner is recognized at Commencement. Also, an honorary lecture called the "Last Lecture" is given annually by a faculty member who is selected on the basis of superior teaching. This is characterized as one of the most prestigious acts of recognition in the University. Lucrative new teaching awards have been instituted at the University of California at Davis. Taylor University (IN) uses classroom teaching excellence as the first and foremost criterion for the selection of the Distinguished Professor Award. The SUNY system has adopted system-wide teaching awards. Cornell University provides $500,000 annually for instructional and curriculum development. Numerous institutions have established outstanding teaching awards, week-long celebrations focusing on teaching, and conferences that address undergraduate instruction.

## Ideas for Action

These initiatives illustrate positive movement to improve the rewards and types of recognition for excellent teaching. The reported perspectives of chief academic officers and the general attitudes of faculty members suggest the needs to be addressed are great. A concerted nationwide effort is needed to:

- •Establish an instructional evaluative base that supports a diverse teaching recognition program -- strengthen the commitment to all efforts involved in the teaching evaluation process, utilize existing research to implement new evaluative structures, and collect data from all sources and on all aspects of the instructional continuum that contribute to teaching excellence.

- •Develop internal campus structures that recognize teaching excellence on a par commensurate with its importance -- reallocate resources to balance support for instructional and curricular development and research and grant activity, recognize individuals who demonstrate outstanding accomplishment in a holistic sense of teaching excellence, and reward individual successes in the subcomponents of the definition of teaching excellence.

- •Review existing structures to ensure internal consistency in the application of expectations for outstanding teaching -- maintain high and consistent expectations across all recognition structures, use different rewards to promote achievement in a broad array of areas, and develop both formal and informal mechanisms to promote teaching excellence.

- •Create a proper balance between institutional efforts to promote teaching excellence and other activities (research, athletics, grants, etc.) that are typically associated with institutional pride -- use assessment data and student/faculty accomplishments to promote teaching; host regular events on undergraduate education, teaching excellence, and general education that demonstrate institutional commitment; and integrate teaching excellence into normal media releases and public relations efforts.

## Leadership Opportunity

The entire gamut of employment-related processes represents the most tangible arena where academic leaders can assault the weak underpinnings of teaching. At each step where a personnel decision is made (hiring, promotion, tenure, merit, etc.), academic leaders have an opportunity to affect the importance of teaching. Teaching competence can be measured in a far more effective manner in the initial hiring stage. Annual review procedures can incorporate in a more substantial way assessments of teaching and scholarly competence. Promotion, tenure, and recognition processes afford countless opportunities for reinforcing the significance of effective instruction.

While these issues are the most obvious areas of reform, they are also the most volatile. Traditions run long and deep. Perceptions are weighted on both extremes. The issues are many and varied. The liabilities and hazards are many, but the call for leadership cannot be ignored. Administrative and faculty leaders must assess their campus to determine the starting point. They must come to agreement on objectives to be achieved, steps to be taken, and outlines to be followed. This chapter suggests countless alternatives; they cannot all be achieved at one time. Step-by-step and year-by-year, a campus can achieve its desired level of teaching commitment!

---

*The liabilities and hazards are many, but the call for leadership cannot be ignored. Administrative and faculty leaders must assess their campus to determine the starting point.*

---

# Chapter Seven

## STRATEGIC ADMINISTRATIVE ACTIONS

The area of strategic administrative action provides academic leaders with a broad range of opportunities to support teaching. Strategies that incorporate an emphasis on teaching range from the most basic and routine activities to highly sophisticated, planned efforts that affect the entire campus. The latitude this area provides presents unmatched flexibility for the creative leader to utilize personal initiatives and innovative efforts. While the opportunities for action are endless, strategic actions that support or promote teaching do not happen spontaneously on a regular basis. They require sustained effort, hard work, and, often, calculated planning to ensure their effectiveness.

Strategic administrative actions require planned initiatives that are designed to affect the campus in a specific manner. Countless strategies exist that might be put in place. One might simply use an "opportunity knocks approach" to introduce the importance of teaching, to emphasize student success, or to recognize faculty achievement. When used on an occasional basis in a hit-or-miss fashion, it is not a strategic action. But, if it is used as a planned strategy to influence the campus, it can be utilized as an effective technique. This approach, however, does have some drawbacks. For example, care must be taken so actions are noticed and don't get lost among other issues. Actions of this type are often perceived as one person's efforts and thus have limited institutional impact. Also, if one is not careful, such actions can give an impression that teaching is of only modest importance. When the "opportunity knocks approach" is used as a singular mode of operation, its effectiveness is typically limited. It may be used as an initial strategy, but it is usually most effective when combined with other strategies, thus becoming an integral component in a larger campus-wide effort.

A somewhat higher order of planned action is the "leadership initiative approach" which requires the chief academic or executive officer to assume more of a role as a teaching administrator. Teaching in this sense does not occur in the traditional classroom. Rather, the actual teaching occurs in the President's Council or Council of Deans. Through such forums a management philosophy of instructional effectiveness is actually taught to other administrators. The teaching agenda can then be transmitted throughout the campus in the minutes of administrative meetings. Team building concepts can be introduced and coordinated in a planned manner. The integral nature of teaching can be fostered on a daily basis as the discussions continue in the various councils and units of the campus. Strategic actions of this type can evolve into memos or position papers on teaching. Such agenda items can serve as the bases for faculty conferences or administrative retreats. Formal and informal initiatives of this type can place teaching and other instructional topics as a primary agenda on campus.

*Special care must be taken in such efforts to emphasize teaching, for changes will not occur without specific direction.*

A third, and more complex, action is the "team building approach". This strategy incorporates concepts from the "opportunity knocks" and the "leadership initiative" approaches and extends them throughout the entire administrative structure. Team-building activities typically require some type of written plan, since administrators outside the academic areas (e.g., business, student services, public relations) are asked to "buy in" to concepts and ideals that are new or may seem unrelated to their primary roles. Essentially, administrators throughout the institution are asked to emphasize teaching whenever it is possible. This may occur by something as simple as adding a few sentences to a news release or adding a teaching component to a major grant. Or, the director of the physical plant may be asked to give special attention to the condition of classrooms on campus. Special care must be taken in such efforts to emphasize teaching, for changes will not occur without specific direction. The analogy of asking the chemistry professor to introduce writing-across-the-curriculum may serve as an excellent example. Without specific assistance, probably little will occur. The first step in such a process might be to involve staff members in public relations, student services, news services, grants and alumni relations. The commitment demonstrated by vice presidents and directors in non-academic areas is highly critical to the success of this approach. The experience of a dean of instruction at a liberal arts college in the Midwest illustrates some of the conflicts present when other administrators are not supportive of the instructional mission:

> The top level administrators at this college have very little teaching experience and other than myself, no research or scholarly background. The President, the Business Officer, the Development Director, and the Admissions Director are all individuals who have no classroom experience whatsoever. I am the only member of this administrative team who holds an earned terminal degree and, I hope it is appropriate to say, the only one who has an identity with an academic discipline in which he actively participates.

> My purpose in relating this is not to "toot my own horn". It is simply to point out that one important institutional result of this collective lack of academic experience is that this senior team has difficulty understanding and relating to the teaching faculty. There is therefore a long history of important decisions being made with little reference to or understanding of their impact on the faculty. This, over the years, has produced a demoralized faculty.

> The President brought me to the administrative team at least partly because he knew there was a problem of faculty morale and felt that a dean with my background and perceptions might be able to address the problem.

> I have been able to address it. However, without the support of the other senior decision makers on the administrative council, I cannot implement solutions. Small changes have been made and they have borne results. Substantive changes, however, are resisted by my cabinet colleagues so the problem persists. It is a deeply rooted problem relating to the values and ethos of the institution.

> I used to think that the value of teaching experience and terminal degrees is exaggerated in assessing qualifications for college and university

administrators. After all, administration is largely "people work" and we all know former professors with Ph.D.s who are incompetent as Deans, Vice Presidents, or Presidents. I don't feel that way any longer. I think that I now see the value of teaching and scholarly experience and of the terminal degree. Among other things, such credentials help one identify with and understand the people one leads. It is my conviction that effective administrators need such experiences and credentials to do their jobs competently.

A final example of how a strategic action may be used to elevate the role of teaching on campus may be illustrated by the "major thrust approach". Like the other initiatives, the "major thrust approach" incorporates concepts fundamental to each of the previously described approaches. In this case, however, the agenda to promote teaching is integrated within a major campus-wide thrust or project. In this way, teaching is promoted either directly or indirectly through the use of another medium. Here, too, there are numerous alternatives. One might, for example, develop a project that incorporates the concepts proposed by Patricia Cross (5) of integrating student research activities into the classroom. The integration of teaching and research has tremendous potential for the future. Another strategy might be to utilize a campus-wide initiative like student outcomes assessment to stress the importance of teaching and learning (15). Alverno College (WI) and Northeast Missouri State University serve as excellent examples in this regard. East Texas State University has used a television and satellite technology project to bring new information and insights to the campus instructional program. Still other institutions have simply identified teaching as their primary agenda and have grouped other projects under the theme of "undergraduate education."

## Supportive Nature of Strategic Administrative Actions

Without question, strategic administrative actions are the easiest way for an administrator to demonstrate a commitment to teaching. Typically, there is wide latitude for action in this area, for normally it does not impinge on faculty prerogatives or institutional policies. Besides, faculty members will typically embrace positive comments and initiatives regarding teaching from the administration. Unless the teaching thrust is connected with a massive new effort, the costs associated with most strategic actions can be minimal.

Rhetoric is cheap! Administrators must go beyond the elementary level of simply making positive statements about the importance of teaching. Strategic administrative actions that foster teaching excellence require an action-oriented commitment. A high level of energy is needed to sustain action over a long period of time. Plans are required that promote the teaching agenda on various fronts. Continuous efforts are needed to ensure that teaching is given high visibility in press releases, research projects, promotional materials, and innovative efforts. Strong positions are required to implement teaching as an integral component in the faculty employment, promotion, tenure, and reward structures. Supportive actions are needed to promote and encourage curriculum development activities that extend beyond traditional departmental interests. The development of sophisticated teaching evaluation strategies require massive administratively driven action.

Table 10 vividly illustrates the need for extraordinary action on the part of most administrators if teaching is to receive increased attention. Noting that there is "lots of room for improvement" grossly understates the need. The only statement in the survey to reach the 8 and above standard of good/excellent was that of emphasizing teaching in speeches and presentations. Even so, this is the least tangible and probably the least action-oriented statement of the category. The mean rating of 5.8 on the use of news releases and articles emphasizing teaching illustrates that relatively little conscious attention is given to this area. The ratings of 5.4 on the collection of data to improve instruction and the 4.5 on research designed to improve instruction are an embarrassment to the profession. The 14 percent and 23 percent of chief academic officers rating these items at the good/excellent level represent a serious indictment of the professoriate and suggest an appalling lack of interest in organized efforts to improve instruction. Forty-two percent of the chief academic officers rate the use of research to improve instruction at the lowest levels. With all of its research, sophistication, and prestige, it is amazing that the higher education community is willing to commit so little to teaching excellence. The opportunities for leadership initiatives in these areas are almost unlimited.

On a composite basis, chief academic officers at larger institutions tend to rate the five strategic administrative action items

*Strategic administrative actions that foster teaching excellence require an action-oriented commitment. A high level of energy is needed to sustain action over a long period of time. Plans are required that promote the teaching agenda on various fronts.*

significantly higher than do their colleagues at the smaller institutions. As will be illustrated in the sections that follow, however, much of this added emphasis is derived from the items focused on emphasizing teaching, using news releases and conducting research. These perceptions were validated by materials and unsolicited comments provided by the chief academic officers in the study. There is, for example, a greater use of newsletters that promote teaching at larger institutions than is common on the smaller campuses. Some of these differences are undoubtedly associated with the levels of financial support and the breadth of needs that must receive support in a more diverse setting.

**Table 10**
**Perceived Commitment of Strategic Administrative Actions in Support of Instructional Effectiveness**

| Items | % Rating 1, 2, or 3 | Mean | % Rating 8, 9, or 10 |
|---|---|---|---|
| The importance of teaching is emphasized by upper level administrators in speeches and public presentations | 3 | 8.1 | 73 |
| Academic administrators across campus regularly reinforce the importance of effective teaching | 4 | 7.6 | 62 |
| News releases and articles are regularly used to focus attention on exciting classroom activities | 20 | 5.8 | 28 |
| Institutional data on teaching effectiveness are collected and used as a means to improve instruction on campus | 28 | 5.4 | 23 |
| Research designed to improve the quality of instruction is regularly conducted on campus | 42 | 4.5 | 14 |

*These data represent a serious indictment of the professoriate and suggest an appalling lack of interest in organized efforts to improve instruction. With all of its research, sophistication, and prestige, it is amazing that the higher education community is willing to commit so little to teaching excellence.*

## Teaching Emphasized

The level of visibility given to teaching on a campus can have an important bearing on the general perceptions of faculty toward instruction. The fact that the chief executive officer regularly singles out the importance of teaching in routine activities and suggests its importance on special occasions can directly influence the attitudes of faculty members. If a dean regularly teaches a class, it can be used to illustrate the point that the administration strongly supports the importance of teaching. Public statements about an outstanding instructional achievement of a faculty member, a student's success in a contest, or the outstanding teaching record of a department can serve as important indicators to the campus that teaching excellence is highly valued and respected.

Also, a series of regular campus activities can be used to emphasize instructional effectiveness. Goals and objectives in planning documents can provide direction. Research on student attitudes can be used to suggest overall campus effectiveness. Departmental reviews can be used to gain far-reaching insights into the overall instructional strength of a department. Student outcomes assessment mechanisms can be used to promote the teaching/learning process. Recruitment and promotional brochures can highlight low faculty-student teaching ratios, excellent instructional facilities, student and faculty accomplishments, alumni successes, and other factors indicative of a strong commitment to teaching.

Other than those institutions with an enrollment of less than five hundred, Chart 11 suggests that chief academic officers perceive that a fairly strong commitment is made to the level of emphasis given to instruction across the nation's campuses. While there is solid support for this item, the overall mean rating of 8.1 indicates that stronger efforts could strengthen the level to which teaching is emphasized on most campuses.

## Chart 11
## Impact of Teaching Being Emphasized on
## Instructional Effectiveness by Size of Institution

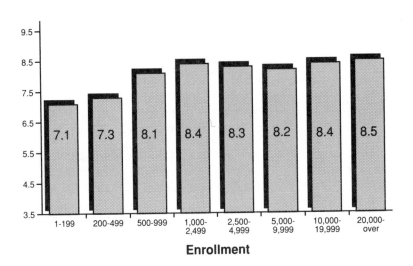

**Enrollment**

There are numerous strategies that might be used to maintain a high level of attention on teaching. For example, the academic dean at Converse College in South Carolina presents a short column in the weekly **Commique** to faculty. The dean has used the "Idea Corner" to stress the importance of faculty development, techniques for better teaching, learning theory, and grading. The chief academic officer at Utah State University regularly uses teaching successes in various academic departments to highlight instruction. At the University of Dayton, the Provost regularly publishes a directory on "Faculty Development Opportunities" so faculty members are aware of professional, personal, and instructional development opportunities. The Provost at the University of Pittsburgh recently used a major memo on undergraduate education to emphasize the significant mission of undergraduate teaching at a research university. Among other areas, he stressed the need to improve undergraduate advising, teaching, and learning; to broaden curricular perspectives; and to involve students in faculty research. A dean at a major university in the East reminds all administrators across the nation that the agenda to promote teaching is never ending:

> We are emphasizing growth in quality and reputation. The central administration repeatedly urges

that excellence in teaching needs fostering as much as excellence in research; its efforts are hampered by static nonsalary funding. The faculty is still not fully satisfied that teaching excellence and development rate as highly as does the research counterpart.

## Ideas for Action

The need to emphasize continuously the importance of teaching is before every upper-level administrator. Campus-wide leadership is needed to:

- Review all promotional and descriptive materials to ensure that the importance of teaching is conveyed consistently to all campus constituencies -- maintain a prominent role for teaching in mission and institutional purpose statements and lists of goals and objectives, promote the teaching character of the campus and its overall quality as a learning environment, and use common themes, data and information regarding teaching in all publications.

- Assess the real and perceived perspectives of the level of commitment made to teaching on the campus -- determine the level of any differences that may exist between perceptions of faculty members and administrators, measure the degree to which levels of commitment expressed by upper administrators are actually implemented, and use follow-up instruments with alumni to determine the overall impact of the teaching/learning environment.

- Ensure that campus leaders regularly refer to the importance of teaching in their daily actions -- demonstrate how the integral nature of teaching influences operational decisions, make a special effort to incorporate factual information regarding instruction in to regular discussions and presentations, and utilize the importance of teaching as a major rationale for specific actions taken by the administration.

# Teaching Reinforced

The need for administrators regularly to reinforce teaching excellence requires constant attention. Again, the routine nature of teaching can leave it at the mercy of other pressing agendas -- personnel matters, budget questions, planning requests, curriculum activities, staffing concerns, etc. Of all campus leaders, the department chairperson has the greatest opportunity regularly to reinforce the teaching function. This obligation, however, cannot be handled by the chairperson alone. The same is true for the dean/division director and other academic administrators. Special efforts are needed regularly to remind individuals throughout the institution that excellence in the classroom really matters. A stand taken on a personnel matter in one department or the interpretation of policy can shape the attitudes of individuals across the campus. The context for teaching on campus can be shaped by comments that highlight the importance of teaching made in speeches by upper-level administrators, the inclusion of teaching-related agenda items for dean's meetings, the use of data concerning teaching from assessment efforts, references made to institutional comparisons of instructional resource allocations, and the introduction of new teaching initiatives.

For managers outside the academic division, the demands to promote teaching are even more formidable. The task of "running" the campus is likely to be of greater importance to many than is the responsibility of relating why certain decisions are made. Clearly, the personnel manager's first requirement is to operate a first-class personnel system. The same demands for professional competence are present for the accountant, office clerk, and the grounds keeper. A proper perspective, however, must be cultivated so these employees sense that they are a part of the whole. Each has a role to perform, but the special qualities of working on a campus are different from being employed in some other type of organization. Learning transcends all segments of the campus. Vice presidents and directors responsible for service functions outside the academic division carry a special instructional burden. They need to understand and support campus instructional initiatives while at the same time exercising strong leadership in the technical areas they represent. At times these demands may seem to be irrelevant, but all administrators need to maintain a proper instructional perspective of the campus. For example, a classroom renovation is more than a physical plant improvement. The classroom is the location where the primary institutional function is carried out. The importance of a remodeling project, for example, must be viewed on the same basis by all employees, whether one is the user of the classroom or responsible for its improvement or cleanliness.

*Learning transcends all segments of the campus. Vice presidents and directors responsible for service functions outside the academic division carry a special instructional burden.*

Chart 12 reveals that, while chief academic officers at institutions ranging in size from 500 to 5000 have a slightly higher perception, there is a substantial need for improvement in the manner in which academic administrators reinforce teaching on most campuses. Again, this increased level of activity can be achieved through a variety of efforts. Most importantly, the creation of a positive teaching/learning environment requires sustained action over a long period of time.

**Chart 12**
**Impact of Academic Administrator Reinforcement on Instructional Effectiveness by Size of Institution**

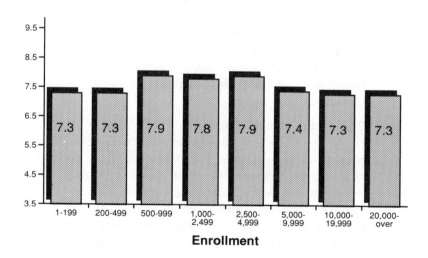

Examples abound of how administrators across the nation try to support the fundamental importance of teaching. For example, at the University of Hawaii at Monoa, the Director of Faculty Development and Academic Support regularly publishes a newsletter entitled **Teaching and Learning** that highlights upcoming teaching-related events, provides suggestions on how to improve teaching, and describes services available to improve instruction. The University of Georgia supports a highly developed Office of Instructional Development that uses its newsletter, **Teaching at UGA,** to give visibility for all phases of teaching. The director of the Center for Teaching and Learning at Southeast Missouri State University regularly teams with faculty members to produce workshops and support materials on such topics as "Making Real on the Promise of Active Learning" and "Using Student Feedback to Improve Classroom Instruction".

## Ideas for Action

These and other examples serve as constant reminders that it is imperative that all administrators regularly assess their level of commitment to instructional effectiveness. Action needs to be taken to:

- Stress to all administrators across the campus that each has a responsibility to contribute to the overall teaching environment -- ensure that personnel policies reference the fundamental purposes of the institution, reinforce actions taken by support personnel to promote effective teaching, and cultivate institutional pride in the performance appraisals of all employees.

- Ensure that campus initiatives which impinge directly upon teaching take precedence over other projects -- assess the need to complete classroom remodeling projects prior to office renovations; give priority to instructional data needs over routine administrative needs; and review campus priority systems for printing, computer, and other services to ensure consistency with overall campus objectives.

- Develop various approaches that stress the importance of teaching to the campus -- establish a newsletter or regular series of articles that emphasize teaching effectiveness, promote teaching enhancement opportunities and the availability of resources to support teaching, and conduct workshops and host conferences that place additional attention on teaching excellence.

• Demonstrate the integral nature of teaching and the various functions that occur on campus -- illustrate the importance of instructional effectiveness for academic personnel and, whenever possible, on decisions affecting non-academic personnel, review budget allocations in terms of their contributions to the instructional effectiveness of the campus, and assess the extent to which instruction is conveyed as an institutional priority.

## Teaching Promoted

The tangible ways in which teaching can be promoted are limited only by one's imagination. Yet, the overall assessment by chief academic officers in this area is relatively low. Like so many other areas, the promotional aspect of emphasizing teaching effectiveness requires a sustained effort. The level of commitment needed to give high visibility to the importance of teaching requires more than an occasional article or paragraph in a recruitment brochure. Rather, it requires a strategically planned set of actions.

Those responsible for the production of news releases, articles, and publications need to understand and report the institution's posture on teaching. They need factual information and may require specific instructions to emphasize the institution's instructional priority. They need ideas for stories that will strengthen the institution's teaching identity. Like any other promotional activity, an effective effort to promote teaching requires a plan of action. Specific directions or objectives are needed. Distinctions need to be made between target groups -- general public, alumni, faculty, students, etc. Timelines need to be developed, areas of responsibilities delineated, and assessment strategies planned. If the campus is lacking in qualified personnel, an outside consultant may be needed to stimulate ideas for possible action.

As part of this effort, the executive leadership team needs to decide what general teaching theme will be emphasized and how factual information will be integrated in to the promotional materials. For example: Will entering student test data be used? What student successes will be promoted? Will student retention data be utilized? Will faculty achievements, recognitions, and awards be emphasized? Will comparisons be made between national funding levels for the institution, various disciplines, or the library ? Will faculty-student instructional ratios be emphasized? Will successful alumni be used to promote instructional effectiveness? Will references be given to faculty credentials and/or the proportion of full/part-time faculty members? There needs to be a clear understanding of the data and information to be used in this process.

---

*Those responsible for the production of news releases, articles, and publications need to understand and report the institution's posture on teaching. They need factual information and may require specific instructions to emphasize the institution's instructional priority.*

---

Chart 13 illustrates that most chief academic officers think their campuses are woefully lacking in the ability to promote the instructional effectiveness of their programs. The problem is of even greater magnitude at campuses with an enrollment under 500.

**Chart 13**
**Impact of Teaching on Promotional Activities on Instructional Effectiveness by Size of Institution**

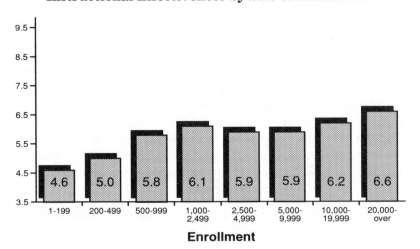

**Enrollment**

108

Promoting teaching can be an effective means of recognizing faculty members for their dedication to excellence in the classroom. Teaching merit award recipients can be highlighted in formal publications and recognition ceremonies. The local newspaper (or in-house publication) might carry a monthly article on one of the outstanding teaching faculty members. New instructional strategies, curriculum initiatives, and classroom research efforts serve as other sources of information that can be used to enhance the level of teaching on campus.

## Ideas for Action

Theoretically, every campus has a list of successes that may be incorporated into the institution's promotional efforts. In summary, there is a need for:

- A formalized plan of action that provides direction for the campus-wide initiative to promote excellent teaching -- charge public relations and news/media personnel with the specific responsibility to emphasize instructional effectiveness, develop a consistent set of facts/information about teaching excellence, and integrate the instructional effectiveness theme, whenever possible, into the regular promotional effort.

- Faculty members to assume a leadership role in writing about and presenting their teaching successes -- promote the development of articles that highlight instructional innovations and experimentation, encourage action-oriented presentations that emphasize teaching excellence and disciplinary competence, and support instructional efforts that provide student involvement in research activities.

- Concerted efforts that identify people-based and factual-based assessment information about the institution -- establish means to identify "teaching successes", faculty/student accomplishments, and other items of human interest; collect data through institutional research efforts that demonstrate instructional effectiveness, and review regularly news items to determine how the teaching theme can be introduced.

• High visibility to be given those items that promote the quality and successes of the institution -- promote teaching awards, recognition, and accomplishments; use assessment data to promote the basic instructional function; and develop human interest stories from students and alumni that give tribute to instructional successes.

## Teaching Researched

As suggested in previous chapters, the opportunities to combine teaching and research are unlimited. There are countless ways in which classroom research can be used to advance knowledge and, at the same time, disseminate new knowledge. The false dichotomy between teaching and research must be set aside. Research on teaching in specific disciplines is a field that remains virtually untapped. Research on teaching can serve as a significant means for self-improvement. Departmentally based research efforts can be used to validate the appropriateness of particular instructional techniques. Cross-departmental projects can be used to assess the amount of learning gained and the interrelationships between certain subjects.

While some positive strides have been made in assessing college student learning, most attempts to research college teaching have been simplistic and superficial. Patricia J. Green and Joan Stark (11:19-20) recently characterized the field as being underdeveloped and inadequate:

> The entire field of research on college teaching is underdeveloped. While attempted improvements in practice proceed by trial and error in scattered settings, little basic knowledge about the process of teaching is available to inform us about the potential impact of intervention through changes in the way teachers teach.

> Basic research that holds promise of improving college teaching and learning needs greater support, broader field testing, and improved translation for the use of institutional researchers. It is no secret

that much of this research originated as psychologists explored various aspects of personality and cognition with the handiest subjects, college students. Colleges themselves have never invested heavily in the research and development enterprise deliberately to improve teaching. Societal interest, as well as institutional self-interest, makes this a propitious time to foster greater amounts of such research.

The perceptions of chief academic officers fully validate the proposition that very little research on teaching is conducted on college campuses. The 4.5 composite mean score for this item was the lowest among the twenty-five surveyed items. Chart 14 reveals that there is practically no research on teaching being conducted at the smallest institutions, and the largest institutions (mainly the "research" universities) have only a limited amount of research focused on teaching.

**Chart 14**
**Impact of Research in Teaching on**
**Instructional Effectiveness by Size of Institution**

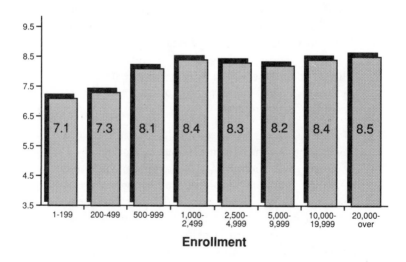

The lack of research on college teaching raises serious questions about the academic integrity of the professoriate. It demonstrates a fundamental weakness in the instructional modes used on campuses throughout the nation. It raises major concerns over the basic commitment to learning. It illustrates the limited knowledge that most professionals have about their own profession. Further, it raises a question as to the overall commitment to teaching by the academic community.

---

*The lack of research on college teaching raises serious questions about the academic integrity of the professoriate. It demonstrates a fundamental weakness in the instructional modes used on campuses throughout the nation. It raises major concerns over the basic commitment to learning.*

---

## Ideas for Action

For most campuses, the question immediately ahead is where to start in forming a commitment to study college teaching. Early initiatives are needed to:

• Improve the knowledge base of faculty members on the findings of research on college teaching -- create a regular campus-based mechanism that facilitates the sharing of research findings, encourage faculty members to conduct research in their own disciplines, and take steps to attempt to narrow the gap between general research on college teaching and specific campus efforts.

• Modify existing structures so they promote higher levels of research on normal teaching activities -- encourage professional disciplinary associations to assume a more active role in promoting research in the field, review promotion and tenure policies to ensure that research on teaching is identified as a legitimate and desirable scholarly activity, and use rewards and recognition to encourage the development of instructionally-based research.

• Stimulate research activity as a campus-wide teaching initiative -- integrate classroom research activities as a regular part of the student's learning experience, encourage experimentation (individual or department) on various instructional strategies, and promote team-teaching experiences that combine successful instructional techniques in one discipline with those of another.

## Teaching Analyzed

Another major weakness of higher education is its unwillingness to collect and analyze data for the purposes of improving instruction. The evaluation of instruction for the purpose of instructional improvement is besieged by many of the same issues raised when teaching evaluations are used for the purposes of a personnel action. When the word evaluation is introduced, "red flags" go up. While such reactions are understandable, the question of evaluation can no longer be neglected. The dual nature of this issue (self-improvement vs. personnel action) must be separated. Instructional improvement must be a continuous process. There is a need to collect student data and other forms of information about instruction on a regular basis. Diagnostic processes need to be established so instruction can be evaluated in an analytical manner, and support systems providing for follow-up consultation and self-improvement need to be implemented. Efforts of this type receive further attention in Chapter 9.

---

*When the word evaluation is introduced, "red flags" go up. While such reactions are understandable, the question of evaluation can no longer be neglected.*

---

In addition to individual faculty evaluations, departmental reviews can serve as another source for assessing instructional effectiveness. Outside curriculum consultants can be used to assess the up-to-date nature of the departmental curriculum. National accrediting bodies can often aid in this process. Input from current students and follow-up studies of alumni can add to individual and departmental teaching data-bases. While these sources will not likely identify new problems, program evaluations commonly spotlight and facilitate action on matters that need an extra or outside push. Departments can also be the source of important instructional research projects that span several sections of the same course.

The need for systematic approaches to these institutional data collection processes is obvious. Again, Green and Stark (11) emphasized the need for campus-wide efforts:

Institutional research, a little publicized aspect of university operation, typically has focused on aspects of organization most closely allied to funding, facilities and enrollment planning, systems operations, and report generating. In relatively few universities are personnel in the institutional research office either appropriately trained or inclined to apply basic research to the improvement of teaching and learning. In some universities, a separate office of faculty instructional development also exists. In these offices too, neither the origin of the developmental activity nor current expectations are likely to foster research directly concerned with teaching and learning. It is time for these offices to broaden their mission to include the translation and field testing functions as well as the training of faculty members to be classroom researchers.

Chart 15 points out that, as perceived by chief academic officers, it is necessary to improve dramatically the collection of data for instructional improvement purposes across all institutions. Progress in this area could strengthen the commitment to instructional effectiveness.

**Chart 15**
**Impact of Teaching Data Collection on**
**Instructional Effectiveness by Size of Institution**

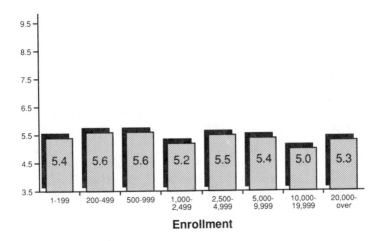

**Enrollment**

# Ideas for Action

A series of strategic administrative actions is needed to integrate the systematic collection of teaching data into the basic structures of higher education.This initiative can be started by:

- Delineating instructional improvement as a high priority for the institution -- make a clear distinction between self-improvement and personnel related needs in the campus data collection procedures, elevate the importance of instructional development activities, and reward departmental initiatives that promote instructional improvement.

- Promoting the development of campus-wide data collection processes that encourage instructional development activities -- encourage the establishment of procedures that recognize disciplinary distinctions and variations in instructional methodologies, develop specific statements designed to assess and improve instruction, and design instructional research procedures around the instructional improvement effort.

- Utilizing a variety of sources to assess and improve the level of instruction provided on campus -- encourage departments to devise their own initiatives to improve instruction; incorporate teaching assessment as a regular departmental review item; and use consultants, advisory committees, and other outside agencies to improve the quality of the instructional program.

- Building campus expertise in the instructional improvement process -- encourage the effective use of data collection procedures, develop faculty ownership in the instructional assessment and development process, and identify individuals on campus that have specific capabilities and responsibilities to assist in the instructional assessment process.

## Leadership Opportunity

Academic administrators have an unlimited opportunity to make a significant impact on their campuses through the use of strategic actions. As implied by the word "strategic", actions must be calculated, organized, and carefully planned in a manner to translate words into action. Excellent teaching does not occur in isolation.

This chapter vividly illustrates the wide variety of approaches available to emphasize, reinforce, and promote effective teaching. Many of these alternatives are low cost and only require a concerted effort. Others demand collaborative actions by individuals throughout the administrative structure. Regardless of the initiative, it is imperative that administrators assume the leadership role. Faculty colleagues need various demonstrations of action to be assured of the commitment to teaching.

Strong administrative efforts to stimulate and highlight teaching excellence are intermediate steps to the process of researching and analyzing teaching. The professoriate has obviously neglected this essential element in the teaching/learning process. Goals and objectives need to be clearly stated before substantial gains can be achieved in these areas. The collection of data on teaching and campus-wide efforts to research teaching need to be carefully planned. The relationships between research and faculty evaluation (real or perceived) must be articulated in a manner to achieve the goals of both initiatives. This agenda must be addressed!

---

*As implied by the word "strategic", actions must be calculated, organized, and carefully planned in a manner to translate words into action. Excellent teaching does not occur in isolation.*

---

# Chapter Eight

## INSTRUCTIONAL ENHANCEMENT EFFORTS

The level of commitment an institution makes to support its instructional programs is difficult to measure since enhancement efforts take various forms. As already suggested, the campus environment, employment policies, and administrative actions can dramatically influence the real and perceived nature of instruction on a particular campus. In a similar manner, the improvement mechanisms used to enhance and strengthen instruction can shape faculty opinions and attitudes. Like so many other aspects of teaching, however, instructional enhancement efforts require a substantial increase in the amount of time and energy devoted to these activities. Even after the commitment has been made, without continual administrative attention, the perceived level of support can quickly erode. As noted by an academic dean at a western college, broad-based action needs to be taken:

> It is clear to me that **much** needs to be done to "put our money where our mouth is". As a small liberal arts college, we stress effective advising and engaged teaching. We **have** to find more effective ways of rewarding and fostering such things; even when tangible support ($!) is not there, intangible support can mean all the difference. More peer contact -- both within and across the disciplines -- is something I'm working hard to create.

One of the most fundamental ingredients in all enhancement efforts is the level of commitment given to these improvement mechanisms. Institutional support is critical, but most enhancement efforts do not require large amounts of resources. They do, however, need to be guided by a strong commitment to four basic principles. First, teaching must be granted equal access to existing programs designed to enhance the research and scholarly competence of the faculty. Efforts need to be undertaken to integrate the complementary nature of scholarship and teaching. Existing programs need to be modified to facilitate this expanded philosophy, or new parallel programs that emphasize instruction need to be established. Sabbatical leave programs, special grant programs, and recognition efforts need to be available to promote teaching as well as scholarship. Second, there needs to be a balanced commitment to teaching and scholarship. Each institution must, of course, determine what the proper balance will be. This decision must be based upon a thorough review of the institutional mission and an analysis of the actual resources dedicated to current research and grant functions. The proper balance should not be interpreted as meaning equal dollars, for in the vast majority of cases, the commensurate portion of funds needed to support the teaching function will greatly exceed those needed for the research function. Third, since no single approach will meet the instructional enhancement needs of the faculty, programs need to include a broad array of enhancement approaches. Programs should encourage and facilitate curricular change, instructional innovation, classroom experimentation, instructional improvement, assessment and evaluation, student success and learning, etc. Institutional efforts need to include various alternatives (leaves, grants, stipends, etc.) that are based at the department as well as institutional levels. Fourth, a high level of visibility must be given to the enhancement efforts, since the importance of teaching can often get lost in the other events of the institution. Besides, as noted previously, academicians have an amazing propensity to lose sight of the positive and dwell on the negative. The level of funding to support instructional enhancement efforts needs to be emphasized. The number of alternatives available to faculty members and the opportunities for instructional improvement need to be stressed.

---

*The proper balance should not be interpreted as meaning equal dollars, for in the vast majority of cases, the commensurate portion of funds needed to support the teaching function will greatly exceed those needed for the research function.*

---

# The Supportive Nature of
# Instructional Enhancement Efforts

In contrast to some of the other administrative initiatives, instructional enhancement efforts provide a direct and tangible sign of the level of institutional support for teaching. This distinction places added importance on the amount of attention and level of resources dedicated to instructional improvement activities. When a faculty member or department is recognized for a significant instructional improvement or a curricular advancement, other members of the academic community take notice. When a colleague receives a special grant or stipend to experiment with a new teaching technique, interest is generated in other segments of the campus. When released time is allocated for an instructional improvement project, a significant symbol is given to the rest of the campus.

Time, energy, and resources allocated to instructional enhancement typically produce multiple effects. They stimulate and encourage the particular individual to move forward, as well as demonstrate administrative commitment to the rest of the campus. Additionally, they generate new levels of creative thought among colleagues for activities they might undertake. New resource allocations can rekindle the intellectual vitality so essential to the well being of the faculty. Special recognitions can provide avenues and opportunities for administrators to make connections between scholarship and teaching. Most important, commitments made to instructional enhancement efforts serve as practical means to improve instruction.

---

*Time, energy, and resources allocated to instructional enhancement typically produce multiple effects. They stimulate and encourage the particular individual to move forward, as well as demonstrate administrative commitment to the rest of the campus.*

---

With all of these positive attributes, one might assume that instructional improvement activities on most campuses would be of high importance. Table 11 suggests just the opposite. The chief academic officers gave low ratings to all of the items in the category. As a group, only the instructional development items (described in Chapter 9) received a lower composite rating. While academic leaders at the larger institutions (above 2500) tended to rate those items slightly higher, the differences for the entire category were not significant at institutions of varying enrollment. All of the items are clearly rated at a level that suggests the need for massive improvement.

### Table 11
### Perceived Commitment of Instructional Enhancement Efforts in Support of Instructional Effectiveness

| Items | % Rating 1,2, or 3 | Mean | % Rating 8, 9, or 10 |
|---|---|---|---|
| Funds are available to support instructional improvement items (e.g., conferences on instructional effectiveness, faculty development activities, and other instructional improvement items) | 10 | **7.0** | 49 |
| Curriculum development activities are given high visibility to illustrate their importance | 13 | **6.5** | 40 |
| Administrators regularly emphasize the ways research and scholarly activity can be used to reinforce or support effective teaching. | 17 | **6.1** | 34 |
| Released time and financial awards are used to promote teaching improvement | 20 | **6.0** | 33 |
| Librarians are used to promote effective instruction on campus | 28 | **5.4** | 26 |

None of the items achieved a good/excellent rating from a majority of the chief academic officers. The overall mean scores indicate that there are tremendous opportunities to bring about change in this category. Furthermore, most of these items do not represent politically sensitive or emotionally-charged areas. Efforts in this area can be initiated without a massive investment of time. Also, these items suggest prime areas where significant inroads can be made with a limited amount of new resources. Faculty interested in making changes can be cultivated, instructional advancement can be stimulated, and renewed vigor can be brought to the campus through expanded efforts in this area.

## Emphasis on Scholarship

One of the potential pitfalls of any major campus effort to elevate the importance of teaching is the perception that somehow scholarship is no longer important. Obviously, this is not the case. First-rate scholarship is a requirement for all faculty members, but it does not need to be defined by the narrow "publish-or-perish" syndrome of the past. Faculty members can display some aspects of their intellectual vitality through the demonstration of outstanding instructional competence, the development of new instructional materials, the integration of current concepts from the disciplines, and the assessment of student learning. When classroom research strategies are combined in this setting with other outside scholarly activities, the false dichotomy between research and instruction begins to diminish. Faculty members are thereby freed from the traditional either/or dichotomy and can focus on their primary instructional responsibilities.

Chart 16 indicates that chief academic officers sense that they have not effectively emphasized the integral nature of scholarship and teaching. Academic leaders at the larger institutions (over 20,000) feel somewhat more comfortable with institutional actions in this area, but substantially more attention to this item is needed at all institutions.

**Chart 16**
**Impact of an Emphasis on Scholarship in**
**Instructional Effectiveness by Size of Institution**

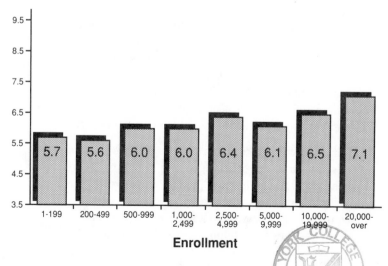

**Enrollment**

121

*First-rate scholarship is a requirement for all faculty members, but it does not need to be defined by the narrow "publish-or-perish" syndrome of the past. Faculty members can display some aspects of their intellectual vitality through the demonstration of outstanding instructional competence ...*

## Ideas for Action

Every administrator needs to delineate clearly his/her own personal perceptions of the relationships between scholarship and teaching before any formal action can be contemplated. In most cases, this intellectual exercise may take several hours and result in a rough statement that matches the institutional mission and articulates well with campus programs. At this point of departure, steps might be considered to:

• Develop a position paper on the integral nature of teaching and scholarship or the need for teaching scholars -- make statements that clearly state institutional directions, encourage classroom and scholarly activity that promotes the integration of the two, and provide numerous examples of ongoing campus activities that illustrate existing efforts upon which to build.

• Review existing procedures and propose necessary changes that would ensure that sufficient options are available to improve instruction -- suggest ways in which existing policies (promotion, sabbatical leave, etc.) could be expanded to incorporate the new emphasis on teaching, propose a philosophical statement that could be used to guide personnel actions, and develop new procedures (when necessary) to support the integration of teaching and research.

• Establish forums to stimulate the philosophical discussion and application of the teaching scholar concept to the campus -- develop statements of philosophy that can be debated in campus meetings and conferences, encourage academic division/department leaders to develop practical examples of how the concept can be implemented, and study ways to modify existing procedures to integrate the new teaching commitment.

## Instructional Improvement Support

The provision of funds to encourage ongoing instructional enhancement activities is the most common and most frequently used form of instructional improvement support. Most institutions set aside at least a small portion of funds to support faculty development efforts and activities that promote instructional effectiveness. Even a modest allocation of funds to support activities in this area can have a significant impact on faculty attitudes. Small grants or awards can demonstrate an action-oriented philosophy that responds directly to faculty requests. While many projects are often highly successful, the fact that improvement projects are supported may outweigh the specific instructional change. On a long-term basis, however, such actions can have a tangible influence on campus-based instructional development activities.

The examples of institutional efforts in this area are numerous. One of several faculty development efforts underway at Worcester State College (MA), for example, is focused totally on instructional effectiveness:

Program of Professional Development: Underlying the program is the principle that professional growth for the individual will benefit the College and its students. The purpose, aims and goals of the program are:

to improve teaching and student advising;

to develop new teaching skills;

to increase a faculty member's command of the body of knowledge that constitutes his/her own discipline, and

to enable a faculty member to develop a command over a body of knowledge in a related discipline.

Participation by faculty is voluntary. Their requests for grants are reviewed by a committee comprised of faculty and administrators who, in consultation with the Vice President of Academic Affairs, recommend approval and allocation of funds. Awards are made for a variety of activities including tuition and fees for continuing education and/or pursuit of advanced degrees; registration fees and travel expenses for attendance at conferences, workshops and seminars; research and publications; educational supplies; and other activities that lead to fulfillment of one or more of the aims of the program.

At Austin College (TX) funds from a Career Development Endowment are awarded annually for faculty activities and projects aimed at their continuing growth and self-renewal. The grants are used to further one or more of the goals, objectives, and plans described in the individual's approved career development plan. Individual and group activities such as the following may be funded.

Research, scholarship, creative activity
Course and training (Certain courses of particular
        relevance, either at an undergraduate or
        graduate level may receive support.)
Special seminars, workshops, institutes
Special conferences and meetings (but generally not
        including routine attendance at professional
        conferences)
Study leaves, sabbaticals
Writing and publication
Faculty exchanges
Visits to other colleges and universities, industrial
        sites, institutions, etc.

At Towson State University (MD) a comprehensive faculty development program offers a series of options for faculty members. Two components that directly support instructional improvement are the Faculty Development/Departmental Enhancement Grants and the Summer Mini-Grants.

## Faculty Development/Departmental Enhancement Grants

Faculty Development/Departmental Enhancement Grants are designed to encourage and recognize faculty and departmental excellence in teaching and scholarship and are specifically intended for faculty self-improvement or renewal. The guidelines for this program are intentionally broad in order to allow faculty to propose innovative and diverse projects in a variety of areas throughout the university. Examples of acceptable proposals include expenses for presentation of papers at national and regional meetings, participation in short courses or seminars, costs involved in retooling into a new area needed in the university, services required to develop unique or innovative teaching methods and courses, and costs involved in the completion of a terminal degree.

## Summer Mini-Grants

The Summer Mini-Grant Program is designed to improve teaching and to give faculty an opportunity during the summer months to spend time working on ways to improve the instructional program at Towson. Funds are provided by the College of Continuing Studies but proposals may be directed toward any segment of the academic program, including day, evening, or summer. Grants are awarded primarily for human services although requests for equipment or supplies will be considered. Proposals must involve improvement of teaching or the curriculum.

While there are numerous programs offered in this area in institutions across the nation, Chart 17 indicates that chief academic officers see the need for substantial additions to the current level of support for instructional improvement items. The composite mean score of 7.0 and the distribution that ranges from 6.3 to 7.4 suggests that there is a need to increase the use of these programs regardless of the size of the institution.

Chart 17
**Impact of Instructional Improvement Support on
Instructional Effectiveness by Size of Institution**

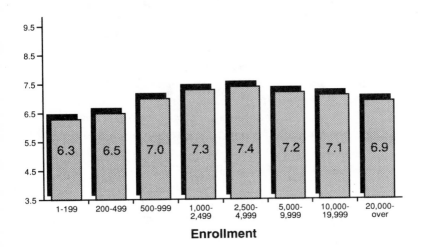

**Enrollment**

## Ideas for Action

Several lessons can be learned from those campuses that have developed a strong commitment to instructional improvements. As a beginning point, there is a need to:

- •Establish a broad-based program that offers far-ranging opportunities designed to improve instruction -- provide guidelines that are flexible so various alternatives can be pursued, develop faculty opportunities for each of the major instructional development areas, and establish the program through a means that cultivates faculty ownership and involvement.

- •Develop programs and procedures that are responsive to faculty needs -- limit the amount of "paper work" required to obtain support or participation, place a substantial portion of the responsibility for the program with the faculty, and use the program as a supplement or enhancement to regular planning or budget priorities.

• Circulate program descriptions, operational budgets, and distribution procedures to the faculty on a regular basis -- describe enhancement opportunities, encourage program use, and highlight program accomplishments.

• Incorporate instructional enhancement efforts into the regular agenda of the campus -- fund instructional items of high priority through the use of enhancement funds, utilize faculty members and other local resources in campus-based activities, host and support campus activities as a regular part of the academic calendar of events.

## Curriculum Development Activities

Curriculum development activities are an important part of the instructional effectiveness continuum. Much of the responsibility for curriculum activity, of course, rests with the faculty who have the primary obligation for its development and implementation. While most administrators are not directly involved in the curricular process, there are several ways in which they can keep the curricular agenda before the faculty.

The curriculum in most cases is in a constant state of change. Its evolving nature requires that specific steps be taken to ensure its viability. Outside consultants are often brought in to validate faculty efforts. Disciplinary accreditation teams are regularly used to review curriculum requirements. Departmental reviews provide still another source to ensure the up-to-date nature and quality of the program. These activities, along with the regular faculty efforts to revise courses, provide a context for the ongoing maintenance of high quality programs. Administrators cannot afford to let these activities go unnoticed. Each event is an opportunity for positive reinforcement of efforts made to maintain a strong, up-to-date curriculum.

Program accreditations, the development of new majors, and substantial program changes provide additional opportunities for visibility on campus and in the community. The care with which curriculum items are handled and the overall effectiveness of the curricular process provide further indications of how instructional improvement is viewed by the campus. While many of these items may seem mundane and routine, each requires regular attention.

The chief academic officer must provide strong leadership in these areas. The level of effective leadership in curricular bodies, the thoroughness of program reviews, and the maintenance of high academic standards are all indicators of the importance of curriculum development activities. The level of institutional support for instructional and curriculum development activities is another important measure of the institution's overall commitment to instructional effectiveness. Institutional resources allocated to this function can be used to reduce the impact of departmental provincialism or to initiate an interdisciplinary program. Commitments to support innovative efforts, for example, can be used to set aside objections to the reform of the general education program. Likewise, small grant programs can be used to stimulate the development of new instructional materials.

---

*The chief academic officer must provide strong leadership in these areas. The level of effective leadership in curricular bodies, the thoroughness of program reviews, and the maintenance of high academic standards are all indicators of the importance of curriculum development activities.*

---

The two most common approaches used to stimulate curriculum activity are the general curriculum development program and the specialized or focused curriculum development program. The course improvement program at Ithaca College (NY) illustrates how funds of this type can be used to support instruction:

### Definition and Objectives

The main objective of this fund is to improve qualitatively the content and methods of instruction at Ithaca College. The fund intends to encourage faculty members to respond to specific academic needs at this institution by:

- refining and updating their teaching skills;

- developing an expertise that contributes to a fuller and more appropriate curriculum;

- developing innovative instructional materials and resources that will be used in existing or proposed courses.

- participating in a workshop provided that such participation has a significant and direct impact on quality of instruction. (Reviewers generally have not considered brief sessions of a professional conference to be a "workshop", but intensive work shops held in conjunction with a conference may qualify.)

To be considered, any proposal submitted to this fund must demonstrate **concrete benefits** to classroom or lab instruction. Faculty are encouraged to discuss ideas or drafts with Committee members beforehand.

The faculty is continually responsible for developing and revising the curriculum. Hence, the IDF funds support activities that are notably innovative or require assistance well beyond those available from school or department sources. The fund is not intended to provide financial support for travel to professional conferences, for equipment, for any other items or activities normally provided for in a departmental or school budget, nor is it intended for use by faculty for personal study in programs leading to an advanced degree. Individual projects may be funded to a maximum of $1200. For projects which require budgets in excess of $1200, additional funds from other sources should be sought. Reviewers often welcome evidence that the Dean and/or department have pledged support to an IDF proposal through travel funding, supplies, or reassigned duties.

Faculty members are invited to submit proposals to the Assistant Provost. Proposals are evaluated according to the following criteria:

1. The project's potential impact on classroom teaching/learning;

2. The project's relevance to curricular and instructional development;

3. The feasibility of the proposed project (likelihood of its successful implementation, justification for attendant costs).

The Lodestar Grant program at Ithaca College (NY) demonstrates the use of a specialized (interdisciplinary) curriculum development program:

### Definitions and Objectives

Students benefit when their teachers are enthusiastic about exploring new ideas and are actively engaged in broadening their knowledge. As the faculty are enriched, so ultimately is the student's educational experience. Whereas IDF grants for direct course improvement focus on curriculum development and pedagogical experiment, Lodestar encourages and supports projects that are interdisciplinary in content. Lodestar projects have as their goal the renewal of faculty members as liberal learners and/or the development of interdisciplinary partnerships. Although immediate curricular impact is not necessary, it is expected that ground work for future team-taught courses and/or interdisciplinary interactions between faculty will result. Note that the program is not intended for use by faculty in degree-obtaining activities.

All proposals are evaluated in terms of the following criteria:

1. The project's potential for enabling faculty members to develop interdisciplinary/multicultural approaches to teaching;

2. The project's potential for integrating bodies of knowledge across the disciplines;

3. The project's feasibility (likelihood of successful completion, justification of costs).

There are various adaptations from these general approaches. For example, the regular curriculum development grants program at the State University of New York at Binghamton was recently modified to give special attention to a new institutional priority -- computer-based instruction.

### Proposals on Computer-Based Instruction:

1. Up to three awards will be reserved for proposals to foster computer-based instruction within the standard curriculum. Proposals for introduction of computer-based material within existent courses will receive priority consideration.

2. Projects may focus on the development of software; of computer-based exercises, texts, or manuals; or informative lectures on computer use and potential in the field.

3. Grants may be used to support summer work, consulting time of Computer Center personnel, the lease of Computer Center hardware or software, travel, or the purchase of supplies.

The general perception of chief academic officers across the nation suggests that a much higher level of attention and visibility needs to be given to curriculum development activities. Chart 18

### Chart 18
### Impact of Curriculum Visibility on
### Instructional Effectiveness by Size of Institution

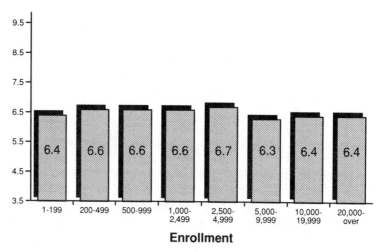

**Enrollment**

indicates that the lack of visibility given to curricular efforts is relatively constant, regardless of institutional size. Substantial improvements are required if this area is to assume the level of attention it deserves.

## Ideas for Action

The need to increase the attention and visibility given to the curricular process is obvious. Its critical nature to instructional effectiveness emphasizes the need to:

- Assess the level of commitment given to instructional enhancement efforts -- review accomplishments gained from the existing programs, assess the program in terms of instructional mission and curricular needs, and evaluate the program with respect to the level of support provided for the program.

- Establish an instructional enhancement program that addresses instructional priorities -- support the use of curriculum development grants; use enhancement grants to meet the broad range of activities, including daily instructional needs and curricular innovations; and expand faculty development which supports instructional development.

- Emphasize the importance of curriculum development through a broad range of activities -- establish curriculum assessment and enhancement as a high priority area in the departmental review process, utilize campus public relations and news/media services to promote curricular change, and recognize and reward individual and departmental accomplishments in this area.

## Released Time and Rewards

It has been an accepted practice on many campuses not to give faculty members released time for the purpose of instructional development. It was typical for academic vice presidents to simply deny such requests on the grounds that such activity was a part of one's normal load and should be done without any special compensation. While much of the former rationale is still intact, the use of released time has increased rapidly over the last decade. The reasons for this shift in philosophy is easy to understand. First, the expertise required to develop some courses places immense burdens on the same faculty members. Second, the rapidity of the change process in some disciplines places additional burdens on faculty members. Third, the interdisciplinary nature of many courses exceeds the normal limits of most faculty members. Besides, the "teaming-up" with another colleague usually requires extraordinary effort. Fourth, teaching specialists demand the same level of support as their research-oriented colleagues.

It is certainly a normal expectation that faculty members assume responsibility for the instructional development activities associated with their areas of instructional competence. Good teachers will continually revise the way they conduct their courses. Changes will continue to result from their own study, reflection, and from talking with colleagues, students, and associates. Nevertheless, it must be recognized that, in a growing number of circumstances, faculty members should be given released time to develop a comprehensive set of new instructional materials, to revise a course, or to propose a new course. Improvement of instruction can no longer remain a shoestring operation. "Assigned time" to bring about specified changes is a significant factor in institutional support for teaching. Such a central undertaking can no longer be assumed as a "normal" expectation of the faculty. Current literature abounds with indications that the profession will experience major faculty recruitment problems in the future. How much better to cultivate the expertise of those already in the profession rather than to force them out of the profession or to diminish their productivity. Traditional "ground rules" must be altered if the profession is to deliver the type of expertise needed in the future.

The same rationale and caution given to using released time can be extended to the use of financial awards. It is questionable whether such awards create a higher level of instructional development activity. They do, however, present clear signals to the campus that recognition can be gained from such activities. In addition to the symbolism associated with such efforts, the use of financial awards is a clear indication to all faculty members that the amount of attention given to instruction is important to the institution.

*Traditional "ground rules" must be altered if the profession is to deliver the type of expertise needed in the future.*

The 6.0 composite mean score given by chief academic officers to the issue of released time and financial awards verifies that the use of such rewards is quite low. There is a general assumption that this level is considerably above the level that might have been expected a decade ago. Chart 19 indicates that while the need to make more extensive use of released time is greater at smaller institutions, the increased use of various rewards is a way for all institutions to make a stronger commitment to instructional effectiveness.

**Chart 19**
**Impact of the Use of Released Time Awards on**
**Instructional Effectiveness by Size of Institution**

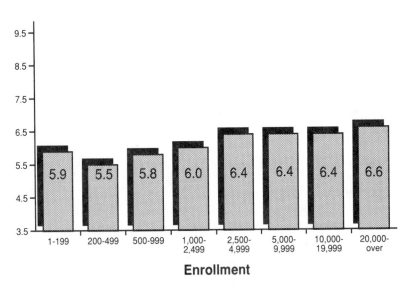

## Ideas for Action

Administrators can demonstrate an increased level of commitment to teaching through the use of financial rewards. Some caution should be exhibited, however, as the institution moves in this direction. Careful distinctions need to be made so as not to detract from the normal and reasonable expectations for faculty to complete regular instructional development activities. While this note of warning should be considered, there is a need to:

- Assess campus practices and develop a program that responds to instructional improvement needs -- establish statements of principle and guidelines, develop priorities to provide direction for the use of the resources and rewards, and fund the program in a manner consistent with institutional needs.

- Provide a reward and recognition program that promotes instructional improvement efforts -- recognize individual initiatives; reward departmental plans and accomplishments; and promote new curricular priorities in departmental areas or campus-wide bases for such items as computer-based instruction, internationalizing the curriculum, writing-across-the-curriculum, or other interdisciplinary activities.

- Review existing faculty personnel policies to ensure that instructional improvement activities are properly recognized -- assess faculty selection processes, review promotion and tenure policies, and develop new programs to respond to areas not addressed by existing policies.

## Role of Librarians

One of the primary responsibilities of the chief academic officer is to maximize the use of institutional resources in support of its educational goals. Regularly, academic deans and vice presidents try to build networks and partnerships across the campus to increase the overall effectiveness of the educational program. While librarians typically serve as an integral academic support unit in this process, they are commonly underutilized as an instrumental resource. Carla J. Stoffle (14:68) emphasized this point in a chapter entitled "The Library's Role in Facilitating Quality Teaching."

> The library becomes an underutilized, expensive storehouse. Librarians are seen as, or what is worse, perform as, keepers of the books, or, in the words of a Cambridge University faculty member, "warehouse managers". Consequently, library materials purchased to support the curriculum lie unused on the shelves. Students who frequent the library often use it as a study hall or as a convenient location for

a social gathering. In addition, when students have a course assignment or research paper that requires the use of library materials, they often perform poorly and spend more time than necessary. The reason for such poor performance is that most students do not have the necessary skills to effectively identify and use appropriate library materials. Compounding the lack of student skills is the lack of informed library involvement in course and assignment planning. This failure to cooperate means that library staff are less effective than they could be in helping students and providing guidance to appropriate materials.

Present-day librarians can do more than simply help students increase their library skills. Many are skilled individuals capable of custom designing course materials and serving as guest lecturers for classes focusing on general or specific research strategies used in areas identified by faculty members. Others can produce custom-tailored bibliographies. Still others are computer and instructional specialists with skills that greatly exceed those of many faculty members.

As Stoffle (14:68-69) suggests, institutions need to reassess the role of their libraries and become more service-oriented. Teaching libraries are needed that demonstrate:

- A commitment to instructing students, faculty, and staff in the effective identification and use of information resources

- A commitment to bringing all library resources to bear on the development of college students into lifelong learners

- A commitment to providing access to and encouraging the appropriate uses of its resources by residents in surrounding communities

- A commitment to developing a climate of learning in surrounding communities by working with other community educational institutions to facilitate the fullest possible use of the information resources available

- A commitment to maintaining a collection adequate to meet basic campus needs

- A commitment to resource sharing so that the campus community has easy access to materials not available in the library

The core component of the teaching library is a bibliographic instruction program -- the systematic instruction of students in effective use of the library resources. The development of a successful instruction program brings librarians into frequent interaction with faculty as they work together to improve the skills and performance of students. Often this collaboration of faculty and librarians takes the form of lectures by librarians to classes with library-related assignments. Sometimes this collaboration is extended to the active participation of the librarian in developing appropriate course assignments to aid the faculty member in attaining the instructional objectives of the course.

Chart 20 indicates that substantial modifications need to be made if librarians are to be used as integral members of the

**Chart 20**
**Impact of the Use of Librarians on**
**Instructional Effectiveness by Size of Institution**

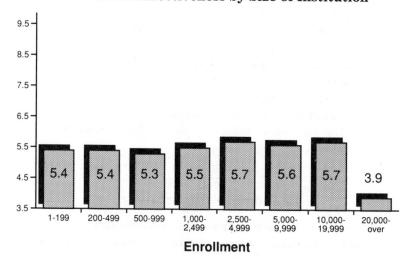

instructional team. The 3.9 rating by chief academic officers at the larger institutions suggests the need to totally reassess their perspectives of the role and purpose of libraries on their campuses.

## Ideas for Action

For all practical purposes, the library stands as a major untapped resource in campus efforts to improve its instructional effectiveness. Significant changes are needed to:

- Reassess the role of the library regarding its fullest capability to enhance the instructional programs on campus -- assess the capabilities of the librarians to determine how they can be used to support academic programs, review instructional resources in the library to determine how it can be used more effectively, study bibliographic instruction activities and other library-based services that might be used to strengthen instructional programs.

- Charge the library director with the responsibility to develop a new instructional statement for the library -- delineate how the library can become a more significant learning resource, outline ways in which closer liaison relationships can be established between the library and academic departments, and promote ways in which the library can be used to enhance instruction.

- Establish the library as a fundamental instructional resource for all academic programs -- utilize librarians on disciplinary-based instructional development teams, assess the existing staffing in the library to determine their effectiveness in addressing campus instructional improvement needs, and use librarians as consultants in the departmental assessment of the up-to-date nature of the bibliographies in existing courses.

## Leadership Opportunity

One might expect that instructional enhancement would be one of the major strengths of American higher education. Yet, chief academic officers rate it as one of the areas of lowest commitment. In some ways, the perception is given that instructional and curriculum development activities reside in the purview of the faculty; therefore, administrative action is inappropriate. Clearly, the faculty carry the primary burden for curricular revision and reform. Unfortunately, it seems that many administrators have totally absented themselves from this area. Admittedly, too, in some cases there is a fine line between what does and does not deserve special support, but that should not preclude positive administrative action.

There is a growing perception that administrators need to take a more active role in curricular activities, particularly in those ways that stimulate, encourage, and foster instructional improvement. While administrators need not interject themselves into the actual curricular process, bold leadership is needed. Aggressive stands need to be taken on curriculum reform agendas. Direct, tangible support needs to be given to innovative, interdisciplinary, and other program development activities. Strong leadership is needed in the area of program review. Through multiple efforts as described in this chapter, the instructional vitality of the campus can come alive. Instructional enhancement can become the vibrant segment of the campus that fosters effective classroom instruction.

---

*There is a growing perception that administrators need to take a more active role in curricular activities, particularly in those ways that stimulate, encourage, and foster instructional improvement. While administrators need not interject themselves into the actual curricular process, bold leadership is needed.*

---

# Chapter Nine

## INSTRUCTIONAL DEVELOPMENT ACTIVITIES

Most campuses maintain some type of a formalized instructional development effort. The size and diversity of these activities, however, vary widely from campus to campus, even among those institutions of comparable size and function. The responsibilities for this effort may be assigned to an individual, a committee, or be housed in an organized unit. Similarly, programs offered on a campus may assume a broad-based character focus or a more limited agenda. Typically, sponsored activities are campus-based, focus on needs identified by campus leaders, and make extensive use of local campus expertise as part of the instructional team.

To provide some guidance for instructional development efforts, Edwin Fenton (10:18-19) identified a set of guiding principles based upon his experiences at Carnegie Mellon University.

> Our experience has led us to identify ten principles which underlie what success we have experienced. These principles, however, must be considered in CMU's context -- a small, research university amenable to change with a President and administrative staff convinced that excellent teaching should parallel excellent research on the part of its faculty. The principles are:
>
> 1. Keep responsibility for good teaching in departments and colleges where it belongs and where it can contribute maximally to the development of a culture of teaching.
>
> 2. Make sure that at least one staff member is an "old hand" with credentials as a researcher and as a grantsperson as well as a teacher.

3. Maintain the active support of key administrators. Consult them often and report personally to them at periodic intervals.

4. Finance your core endeavors with hard money from the University, not with soft money grants which will inevitably come to an end. Make sure that you have discretionary funds so that you can strike targets of opportunity when they present themselves.

5. Enlist the support and active participation of as many faculty members as possible in every aspect of the program. Invite them to plan and lead seminars and workshops and to contribute articles about teaching to your publication list.

6. Don't try to build an empire. Keep a small staff and count on colleagues from the faculty to carry much of the work load, particularly in developing teaching components of their Ph.D. programs.

7. Undertake a new project or two every year while maintaining the old ones at the same time. Choose projects which appear on the agendas of a number of departments and will serve their needs. Aim for variety, a smorgasbord, with something to appeal to every faculty appetite.

8. Provide feedback throughout programs -- to administrators, to faculty members, and to students -- and follow up feedback with support.

9. As you work, keep in mind the major components of a culture of teaching: cultural potency, congruence, continuity, distinctiveness, and clarity.

10. Look ahead toward wider horizons. The concept of a culture of learning offers fruitful possibilities for the future.

Instructional development activities perform a vital role in efforts to shape the instructional character of the campus. Such activities can build a high level of ownership among the faculty, for many are often involved in the specific campus effort. The planned initiatives maintain a visible identity for teaching on the campus. Locally sponsored seminars, workshops, and conferences can be tailored to specific needs and are often more meaningful as they are tied directly to the campus. Activities in this regard have another distinct advantage in that they are almost always aimed at improvement of instruction. This open environment can free faculty members from the threatening nature of regular reviews and allow them to focus on instructional improvement items. A colleague or mentor can often work on this level on a personal basis to deal with difficult problems.

---

*Locally sponsored seminars, workshops, and conferences can be tailored to specific needs and are often more meaningful as they are tied directly to the campus. Activities in this regard have another distinct advantage in that they are almost always aimed at improvement of instruction.*

---

Each campus must make its own decision as to whether its instructional improvement goals are best achieved through a center, office, committee, part-time faculty assignment, or some combination of these efforts. At a small college, responsibility may be placed in the hands of one or two individuals. Or, one may find that a "committee on instruction" is adequate, especially if it has a modest working budget to cover certain basic expenses and purchase reference materials on college teaching, provide "seed" grants to improve instruction, and purchase equipment to demonstrate new resources which support teaching. In whatever form, support must be present and visible. At a large university, a special unit of fifty persons or more may be necessary to provide a comprehensive program of service and research on matters related to teaching -- testing, evaluation, media, learning, course development, and instructional improvement.

Regardless of the approach, faculty involvement is critical to the successful operation of the instructional development activity. Faculty can create a sense of ownership and build a program that serves faculty needs. Faculty participation also helps to counter the perception that traveling experts, technological aids, systems engineers, or even money can provide panaceas for teaching. The improvement of teaching is a responsibility shared by all faculty members.

*Regardless of the approach, faculty involvement is critical to the successful operation of the instructional development activity. Faculty can create a sense of ownership and build a program that serves faculty needs.*

## Supportive Nature of Instructional Development Activities

Instructional development activity serves as an integral component in any campus effort to improve the level of teaching effectiveness. Such campus-based efforts give clear signals to the faculty of the administration's commitment to instructional improvement. The development and use of the local cadre of experts can serve as a vital force in the overall strategy of a campus.

As already suggested, the opportunities for change and improvement in the area of instructional development vary widely. Some institutions have highly sophisticated centers, while others are practically void of such activity. Nationwide, chief academic officers ranked this area as the lowest among the five categories studied. Table 12 illustrates the low level of support for each of the surveyed

### Table 12
### Perceived Commitment of Instructional Development Activities in Support of Instructional Effectiveness

| Items | % Rating 1, 2, or 3 | Mean | % Rating 8, 9, or 10 |
|---|---|---|---|
| Faculty seminars, workshops and conferences on teaching and learning are conducted on campus | 23 | **5.8** | 31 |
| The campus maintains various colleague support mechanisms (mentors, chairperson, monitoring, etc.) to promote and support effective instruction | 21 | **5.8** | 30 |
| Seminars/workshops on teaching are held for graduate teaching assistants | 33 | **5.3** | 27 |
| Effective instruction is promoted by an organized unit or program (e.g., center for teaching & learning) | 36 | **5.2** | 29 |
| Workshops/seminars on effective instruction are conducted for new full-time faculty members | 42 | **4.7** | 20 |

items. Less than one third of the chief academic officers had good/ excellent ratings of items in this area, while a large segment expressed considerable dissatisfaction. There are, however, significantly higher perceived levels of instructional development activity under way in some of the larger institutions. Similarly, institutions with graduate programs are more heavily committed to this area than are those with only undergraduate offerings. Without question, instructional development activities are a vital component that academic administrators can utilize to demonstrate a strengthened commitment to instructional effectiveness.

While the need is great to strengthen instructional development activities, care must be taken to plan carefully the new or expanded efforts. James Eison (9) sets out several warnings to those involved in such activities:

A.  Ignoring institutional context and climate

  1.  Faculty are especially sensitive to institutional context and climate; efforts to initiate personal or institutional change that do not pay close and careful attention to such matters are doomed from their outset (this is especially true when faculty morale is low).

  2.  After identifying its goals and objectives, one of the first tasks a faculty development committee should undertake is an honest analysis of the obstacles and barriers that must first be overcome before these goals can be achieved. Analysis of the forces and resources available to achieve these goals should also be completed.

  3.  Identifying and implementing strategies to capitalize on existing institutional strengths, and to overcome institutional barriers, must become part of the faculty development plan.

B.  Thinking that teaching awards and/or mini-grants are enough

  1.  While recognition and financial rewards can enhance institutional efforts to encourage faculty development, they are, at best, necessary but not sufficient conditions to insure instructional excellence.

2. A useful brainstorming activity a faculty development committee might wish to attempt involves identifying ways to appeal to faculty members' intrinsic and extrinsic motivational forces; whenever and wherever possible, appeals to intrinsic motivation are preferable.

C. Starting off too slowly

1. The start of a new academic year or semester, when morale tends to be high, is an ideal time to announce new faculty development initiatives and activities.

2. Emerson noted, "nothing great has ever been accomplished without enthusiasm;" faculty development programs are no exception. Create ambitious but achievable goals; work visibly and vigorously to achieve them.

3. Insure that all activities and programs have been widely publicized (because faculty do not always read their mail carefully, it is helpful to send out multiple announcements) with considerable advance notice (the people most likely to want to attend a function are often the busiest).

4. One important caution, however, is to not attempt to do too much, too soon. Let your analysis of institutional context and climate serve as your committee's guide.

D. Reinventing the wheel

1. Considerable committee time can be saved by learning about exemplary faculty development programs; though it is unlikely that any program will be perfectly "transportable" to your campus, modifying existing models may be easier than creating original ones.

2. Three sources of information to consult include Eble and McKeachie, **Improving Undergraduate Education Through**

**Faculty Development** (1985), Gaff, **Toward Faculty Renewal: Advances in Faculty Instructional and Organizational Development** (1975), and **Nelson, Renewal of the Teacher-Scholar** (1981).

E. Inattention to quality

1. When provided with high quality programs, faculty members can be an especially appreciative audience; when program quality is poor, faculty can be especially harsh and critical.

2. Thorough and thoughtful planning is one key to help insure quality.

3. When designing programs, remember that it generally does not cost too much more to go first class; faculty will appreciate your efforts and will be more likely to attend future programs as a result.

F. Expecting that all or most faculty will participate

1. Do not anticipate that most faculty will rush to become participants in a faculty development program; this is especially true in the program's early history.

2. Do not judge a program to be a failure if the people who most need help do not initially choose to participate; as with most things in life, many human beings will not openly acknowledge or address problems they know to exist.

3. All faculty can improve their teaching skills; all faculty can benefit from support and renewal. When the best faculty on campus attend your programs, they acknowledge these.

4. When assessing impact, instead of counting faculty participants, estimate the number of students being taught by faculty in attendance.

G. Not using external consultants to maximum advantage.

　　1. External consultants can be used productively to

　　　　a. review program plans and proposals

　　　　b. conduct seminars, workshops and conferences

　　　　c. offer recommendations that may be viewed by others as having greater expertise and credibility

　　2. For best results, the faculty development committee's hopes and expectations must be made explicit and clear to the consultant.

H. Relying on external funding

　　1. To clearly demonstrate institutional commitment to faculty development, it is vital that institutional funding be present to support such activities.

　　2. In addition to using existing institutional funds, thoughtful proposals for new sources of state aide should be developed.

　　3. Though external funding for faculty development programs can sometimes be found (e.g., private foundations, federal programs), these programs are highly, highly competitive (i.e., the likelihood that faculty time and energy devoted to proposal writing will provide funds is very low). Thus, a committee's early efforts should not rely on, or even hope for, such funds.

## Campus Sponsored Activities

Campus-sponsored seminars, workshops, and conferences are used to address a broad range of topics related to teaching and learning. They may focus specifically on teaching, have a disciplinary orientation, or revolve around a campus theme like writing-across-the-curriculum or global perspectives. Similarly, the type of initiative may be narrow or broad in its appeal. For example, many committees have successfully established "brown bag lunches", or other types of informal grass-roots programs to get faculty thinking and talking about good teaching. Such programs tend to attract the interest of a small group of highly motivated faculty who can play a valuable role in supporting other instructional efforts. Others may take the form of a "University Series on University Teaching" as is the case at Ball State University. On an even broader scale is the"Annual Celebration on Teaching" sponsored by Virginia Commonwealth University. This conference brings faculty members from across the campus for a series of presentations and discussions. A new publication entitled **VCU Teaching**, which is a companion publication to the institution's **Research in Action**, has emerged from this elevated role of teaching.

---

*... many committees have successfully established "brown bag lunches", or other types of informal grass roots programs to get faculty thinking and talking about good teaching.*

---

While new initiatives like these are regularly occurring, the chief academic officers note that at the present there is not a strong commitment to these types of activities. Chart 21 reveals that the

**Chart 21**
**Impact of Campus Supported Activities on**
**Instructional Effectiveness by Size of Institution**

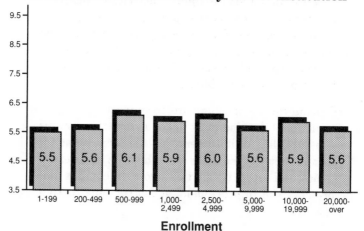

ratings of these academic leaders are consistently low across all institutions.

Several academic leaders noted in the study that an overriding problem they regularly experienced was that many faculty members had no formal preparation on how to teach. Concordia College (MN) and the University of Pittsburgh have offered seminars on college teaching to address some of these concerns. In a short chapter entitled "A Short Course on Teaching for University Faculty Members", David W. Champagne and Margaret A. Waterman (30:99-104) outlined objectives, content, structures, and methods for such a course.

## Ideas for Action

Campus-based programs serve as a tremendous, low-cost vehicle to stimulate interest, build faculty ownership, and address real campus problems. There is a significant need to:

- Involve faculty leaders in the creation of a structure that facilitates ongoing instructional development activities -- develop faculty ownership in the types of programs maintained on campus, establish programs to support campus-wide initiatives and program specific needs, and maintain high visibility for instructional improvement activities.

- Utilize faculty expertise present on campus to support instructional development activities -- host conferences to bring local expertise to bear on new campus programs, develop faculty specialists to assist colleagues in other development activities, and build teams of curriculum specialists to assist in addressing campus-wide problems.

- Provide various mechanisms to support varying instructional development needs across the campus -- establish a unit to serve as the focal point for campus activity, sponsor workshops on a variety of topics, and support activities across the campus that promote the improvement of instructional activities.

# Colleague Support Systems

While not as visible as campus-sponsored activities, departmentally-based colleague support mechanisms provide a strong base for individualized attention. Often these programs are operated on an informal, individual basis and receive little recognition. Many department chairpersons simply assume this responsibility or assign it to a respected colleague in the department. In other cases, more structured programs have been developed. The Academic Dean at Eastern Mennonite College (VA) cites their mentoring program as a major strength:

> One of our most successful programs is the New Teacher Consultant Program whereby a master teacher serves as a mentor and consultant to new faculty. The mentor visits classes, works with the new faculty member on syllabus and test preparation and serves an an encourager and support for the novice. This consultant (on our small campus, one person) is also available to other faculty who may be needing some assistance. Occasionally, as Academic Dean, I refer a faculty member to the consultant for help in evaluating teaching effectiveness and addressing problems which have emerged.

**Goals:**

> To provide support and encouragement to the new faculty member who is striving for teaching excellence in the classroom.

> Through that support to encourage experimentation with different methods and teaching styles to maximize the individual teacher's gifts.

> To provide a supportive context within which to identify strategies for improving teacher effectiveness.

> To assist the new teacher in identifying strengths and weaknesses.

**Structure:**

> While an informal mentoring relationship is encouraged, some structure will ensure that the new teacher is self-consciously engaged with a master teacher

who can share the exhilaration of being successful and encourage in those times of discouragement when "there must be a better way".

1. The new faculty invites the consulting teacher to visit her or his class at least once during the semester.

2. Following the classroom visits, teacher and consultant will meet to discuss the observed strengths and weaknesses. The consulting teacher will work with the faculty member on implementing strategies for increased effectiveness.

3. At the conclusion of the semester, the new faculty shall review the course evaluations (which have been administered in at least two courses) with the consultant. With the consultant's assistance, the teacher shall outline a plan of action in response to the issues raised by students.

4. At the end of the first semester, the new teacher and the consulting teacher will each meet with the dean to evaluate this relationship. A decision will be made at this point as to whether to continue the consultant/new faculty relationship in a structured manner.

5. The teacher consultant shall also be available on an informal basis for such consultation, advice, and encouragement as desired by the new faculty member.

The Collegial Coaching and Mentoring Program at Cardinal Stritch College (WI) provides an extensive set of guidelines for the "coaching partners." This program has clearly stated purposes, identified strategies, stated guidelines, and printed forms and worksheets to guide the process. Other institutions have developed peer observation sessions and course auditing programs so colleagues can actually "sit in" regular classes and then meet with their colleagues periodically to critique the effectiveness of a particular technique or session.

Whether these activities are formal or informal, voluntary or required, Chart 22 reveals that, again, chief academic officers sense a low commitment on their campuses to the use of colleague support efforts to promote effective instruction. Again, there is consistent opportunity for campus leaders to improve the level of support for teaching with little increase in financial commitment.

**Chart 22**
**Impact of the Use of Colleague Support Mechanisms on Instructional Effectiveness by Size of Institution**

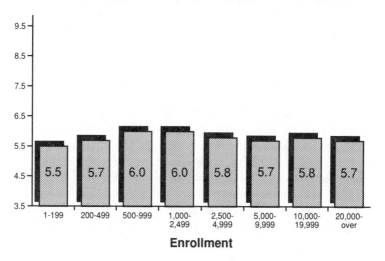

**Enrollment**

## Ideas for Action

Faculty peers have numerous opportunities to assist their colleagues in improving as teachers. To utilize more effectively this institutional resource, plans should be made to:

- Establish a faculty mentoring program for all new faculty members -- demonstrate the institutional priority for instructional improvement; assist colleagues in becoming oriented to academic standards, instructional strategies, and teaching/learning styles; and build faculty instructional teams through the development of cooperative ventures.

- Encourage academic departments to identify strategies that can be used by colleagues to strengthen teaching in the department -- develop disciplinary-oriented teaching seminars, use assessment data to

improve the institutional program in the department, and assess on an individual basis the effectiveness of various instructional techniques.

•Establish mechanisms that will encourage faculty
members to adopt the mentoring concept with other
colleagues -- place a renewed emphasis on self and
departmental improvement, support financially
modest needs to stimulate colleague assessment,
maintain clear distinctions between colleague self-
improvement strategies and personnel evaluative
efforts.

## New Faculty Workshops

Several institutions have conducted workshops for new faculty
members for a number of years. The last five or six years, however,
has witnessed a shift in emphasis in many of the existing programs.
Most of the earlier efforts evolved out of a faculty orientation
program which focused primarily on the sharing of institutional
information to ease the faculty members' transition to campus. In
most cases, it was an opportunity to get acquainted, fill out employment forms, learn about benefits, parking, etc., and be welcomed to
the campus.

Faculty workshops often still cover some of the routine information, but teaching has become the primary agenda in many programs. The four-day program at the University of Buffalo has
integrated a successful microteaching component to complement
four major themes -- course planning, teaching and learning, evaluation, and teaching techniques and faculty assessment. At the
University of Nebraska in Omaha, there are sessions provided on a
philosophy of teaching, student profiles, microteaching, testing and
evaluation, and course planning. At Southeast Missouri State University, a required week-long workshop for new faculty places heavy
emphasis on student learning and strategies for successful instruction as identified by existing faculty members.

Chart 23 indicates that the general perceptions of chief academic
officers reflect a very low nationwide commitment to new faculty
workshops. Again, a significant opportunity is present for academic
leaders to demonstrate the importance of teaching to all faculty
members. New faculty members can hear, firsthand, comments from
campus leaders on the importance of teaching. The mere fact that the

workshop is conducted is another clear signal to the rest of the faculty.

**Chart 23**
**Impact of Workshops for the New Faculty on**
**Instructional Effectiveness by Size of Institution**

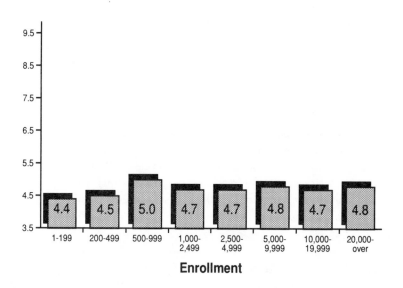

An effective workshop for new faculty members can clearly convey the institution's commitment to teaching excellence; create a positive first impression; develop attitudes, knowledge and pedagogical skills; and build colleague relationships. Like any program, these workshops require a significant level of preparation. Outstanding campus faculty members need to be involved in the workshop, administrators need to support and understand the purpose of the workshop, and topics covered in these early sessions need to address the needs of new faculty members.

## Ideas for Action

To move in a more positive direction, institutions need to:

- Assess the pedagogical competencies of new faculty members and ensure they are properly introduced to the instructional character of the campus -- maintain flexible programs that emphasize essential instructional strategies, delineate campus instructional priorities and expectations, and present data concerning the characteristics of the student body.

• Conduct regular workshops for new faculty members that support the instructional needs of the campus -- maintain a common level of support for the program across all academic units, and focus attention on instructional techniques rather than long-term curriculum development activities.

• Schedule brief instructional sessions throughout the year that build upon the initial new faculty workshop and extend opportunities throughout the year for all faculty members -- build programs that serve the needs of all faculty; give specific attention to instructional concerns unique to the campus; and use these workshops to introduce regularly new instructional concepts and more sophisticated instructional teaching, curriculum, assessment, and research topics.

---

*An effective workshop for new faculty members can clearly convey the institution's commitment to teaching excellence; create a positive first impression; develop attitudes, knowledge and pedagogical skills; and build colleague relationships.*

---

## Workshops for TAs

Increased interest has been sparked in recent years for the provision of workshops for graduate teaching assistants. Pressures from legislators and parents, along with institutional initiatives, have elevated the importance of this area at many institutions. The increasing number of international graduate students also forced some institutions to accommodate their needs. While these early efforts are noteworthy, most training sessions are largely cosmetic and only touch upon some of the most elementary instructional concepts. At a prominent southern university, a day-and-a-half workshop for teaching assistants is voluntary. Participants listen to four lectures and select two sessions from a group of ten. Another major eastern university hosts a Saturday morning session with two lectures and a panel discussion. Few institutions make a major effort to prepare teaching assistants to assume the responsibilities they are given.

The success of these efforts is reflected by a correspondingly low rating by chief academic officers of the extent to which workshops for teaching assistants contribute to the overall effectiveness of the instructional program. Chart 24 reveals that only a few of the relatively larger institutions profess any confidence in the success of these efforts. Major improvements are needed.

**Chart 24**
**Impact of Workshops for TAs on Instructional Effectiveness by Size of Institution**

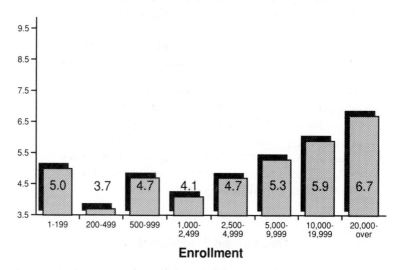

**Enrollment**

There are some serious efforts underway that suggest the future might be somewhat better. At Cornell University a grant from the Exxon Foundation has made possible the development of a four-to-six-week summer program for teaching assistants. Stanford University uses a system of specifically trained TAs consulting with other TAs during the regular year. Carnegie Mellon University has developed a teaching component to be integrated with some of its Ph.D. programs.

# Ideas for Action

For the most part, however, the prospects of dramatically improving the preparation of teaching assistants is fairly limited. If teaching assistants are to be used in the instructional program, action is needed to:

- Develop a list of instructional competencies that must be demonstrated prior to any direct involvement in the classroom -- require the completion of a regular teaching seminar, develop a hierarchy of skills to be mastered and then phase-in teaching obligations, and add a graduate course on college teaching for all teaching assistants.

- Establish teaching competencies as a fundamental requirement in the program of all doctoral candidates interested in a career in higher education -- require teaching and research competencies, provide instruction on teaching and evaluation, and develop skills in course and curricular development.

- Increase the entry teaching qualifications of all individuals involved in providing college instruction -- provide campus-based programs to improve instructional competencies, develop modules and micro-teaching components to be completed, and "phase in" individuals on a step-by-step basis who are involved in providing college instruction.

# Organized Unit/Center

One of the early issues that every campus needs to address is the type of organizational mechanism that will be used to support the instructional development activities of the campus. Clear statements need to be made regarding purposes, budgets, reporting channels, and other routine administrative details. Those responsible for the initiative need to assume a leadership posture that will facilitate efforts designed to improve the overall effectiveness of the instructional program.

Such initiatives can, again, assume a variety of forms. At the University of Scranton, for example, the Office of Instructional Development is guided in its efforts by a set of six goals and thirty-five supporting objectives for the 1988-93 planning cycle. The goals for the Office are to:

Continue to promote the services offered by the Office of Instructional Development.

Increase the quality of teaching at the University.

Provide consultation and interpretation services on use of the student evaluation of faculty form (IDEA).

Raise the awareness level of the importance of quality teaching.

Work with UBUGE and Curriculum 90 committees to implement recommendations regarding faculty development.

Encourage the Office of Instructional Development staff to participate in professional development activities.

The Teaching and Learning Committee at Montana State University follows a much simpler format. Its charge is as follows:

The Teaching/Learning Committee (TLC) is a university-wide faculty committee responsible for promoting faculty development at MSU. TLC's stated goal is to "promote the process of critical and creative thinking with interactive teaching and learning among teachers and students."

The Committee, comprised of faculty members from each college or school at MSU, administers money provided by the academic vice president for faculty development. TLC activities include:

1. Workshops

Workshops on instructional design and methods are held periodically during the academic year and for extended periods in the summer. Faculty often obtain ideas in workshops which are used for subsequent course development work.

2.  Instructional Development Grants

    Competitive grant rounds are usually held twice per year. These grants go to faculty for innovative course development.

3.  Faculty Forums, Seminars and Conferences

    The Committee sponsors or co-sponsors informal and formal faculty gatherings to share or develop ideas on teaching and learning.

4.  Special Projects

    The Committee sponsors a variety of special projects not related to development of a particular course.

At Wabash College (IN), the academic dean reports that the Teaching and Learning Committee provides several important services.

1.  At the beginning of the school year, the committee invites the faculty to attend a symposium at a nearby conference center. A program on a common teaching problem is arranged. For example, this year we worked in small groups on statements about what constituted a good teaching class for each of us. Then we searched for the common elements in each group's thoughts. Second, we tackled four scenarios involving typical tough teaching problems that arise in Wabash courses. Third, a panel of students and senior faculty introduced new teachers to teaching at Wabash.

2.  The committee has sponsored workshops on teaching problems. For example, the comments written by teachers on essays often mean one thing to the teacher and another to the student. The workshop explored these differences and found ways to improve and clarify comments.

3.  The committee has sponsored guest lecturers on pertinent topics. A popular subject for discussion

at Wabash has been the teaching of values in the classroom. It turns out that there are many different faculty opinions on the subject and the speaker was able to help us find common ground.

4. Members of the committee are prepared to help faculty members with their individual teaching problems. The committee members will visit the classroom, they will videotape the teacher at work, and they will discuss their observations with the teacher. This is done in a non-threatening way since administrators do not participate in this activity.

Chart 25 suggests that larger institutions have generally been more active in utilizing a center/unit to continue the overall effort to improve instructional effectiveness. The expression of sporadic and low levels of commitment by the chief academic officers suggests that efforts to establish formal mechanisms have lagged considerably. While there are many very active centers for teaching and learning or instructional development across the nation, there are also numerous institutions that have little or no effort under way.

**Chart 25**
**Impact of an Organized Unit on Instructional**
**Development by Size of Institution**

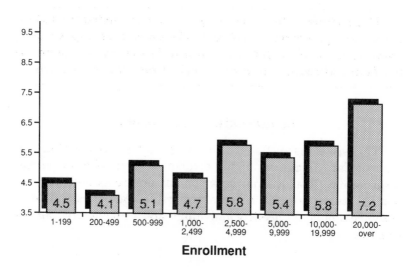

# Ideas for Action

To correct this imbalance, actions should be undertaken to:

- Establish a campus unit that is dedicated to the improvement of instruction -- state clearly the purpose, objectives, and role of the unit; delineate the expectations for the unit and how it fits within the academic structure; and utilize the unit as a catalyst to promote instructional and curriculum development activities.

- Provide an adequate level of support for the unit so significant instructional improvements can be achieved -- establish a physical location for the unit, create staff support with the necessary levels of expertise to operate the program, and fund the program at a level so it can effectively address its objectives.

- Develop a long-range plan that delineates how the institution will move forward in an expanded manner to address its instructional development needs -- assess the needs of the campus to determine strengths and weaknesses, identify long-term goals and objectives to guide campus action, and provide an appropriate level of resources to support the stated directions of the unit.

---

*Regardless of the agreed upon format, instructional development programs need to build upon a strong sense of campus ownership. Activities should be designed around the needs of individuals and academic programs on campus.*

---

# Leadership Opportunity

The type of instructional development activities undertaken on a particular campus are highly diverse. Regardless of the agreed upon format, instructional development programs need to build upon a strong sense of campus ownership. Activities should be designed around the needs of individuals and academic programs on campus.

Administrative and faculty leaders need to assess the campus and its academic personnel in terms of instructional needs. Attention should be given to the needs of teaching assistants, part-time faculty, new faculty, and colleagues who have served the campus over a long period. Workshops and conferences need to be conducted that address substantive campus issues, such as faculty evaluation, general education, instructional strategies, and mentoring.

Similarly, the role of faculty colleagues cannot be overlooked. While the administration needs to be supportive of efforts in these areas, they need not control or monitor all activities. A well designed mentoring program or a set of individually arranged colleague experiences might produce results in some areas that would greatly exceed an administratively-controlled initiative. Individuals on a campus must have a willingness to venture, to pick and choose, and experiment. There is no one initiative that ensures excellence in the classroom, but one positive action that affects each faculty member could strengthen the campus teaching culture.

---

*There is no one initiative that ensures excellence in the classroom, but one positive action that affects each faculty member could strengthen the campus teaching culture.*

---

# Chapter Ten

## LEADERSHIP CHALLENGE

The leadership challenge to re-establish the importance of teaching is one that is shared by all constituencies associated with higher education. Leadership must come from both inside and outside the institution. Many governors and state legislators have already begun to demonstrate great interest in and influence over the internal priorities of public institutions. The assessment movement has raised public awareness of the significance of learning and the importance of demonstrating academic success. Professional associations have assumed new roles in emphasizing teaching and suggesting ways in which it might be improved. These initiatives illustrate only a few of the pressures being applied to academe.

Efforts to restore teaching to its primacy are likely to increase from these and other forces outside the academic community. While such external pressures will continue to influence the academy, the substantive leadership challenge must be met by individuals within it. Again, the obligations are shared by the entire academic community. Students need to insist on quality instruction and push for accountability measures that demonstrate effectiveness in the classroom. Faculty members need to press forward in efforts to ensure the effective evaluation, recognition, and reward of teaching excellence. Departments need to set aside "back scratching" tendencies and vigorously promote outstanding instruction. Committees that have hamstrung genuine curriculum development activities need to be recharged. Policies to promote more effective teaching need to be revised or updated by teams of administrators and faculty members. Finally, and most important, administrators need to reaffirm their commitment to excellent instruction and rechannel their time and energy to items that make a real difference in the quality of teaching and learning on campus.

The agenda is achievable, but such a transformation requires renewed vigor and leadership from administrators across the nation.

Eble (8:84-85) suggests that the long-standing traditions and research forces may be too great an obstacle to overcome. His comments provide a sobering context for the leadership challenges ahead.

Despite the strong liberal arts collegiate tradition, present-day colleges and universities are so influenced by the size and prominence of research universities that little can be expected in arriving at a better balance between teaching and scholarship. Nor is a faculty, pressed as it has seldom been before by an unfavorable academic market, capable of doing much to reverse the tendency of that very market to increase the necessity to publish. If we but had administrators who were informed by other than parochial views and who were willing to exercise the powers they have and the leadership they might exercise. If we but had institutions that represented more than the diffuse self-interests of the faculty and expedient responses to immediate public pressures. If we but had a culture less susceptible to values based on higher and larger. If we but had students more resistant to a faculty's tendency to replicate themselves and to carry out an institution's pressure for productivity. Even then, we would still not be free of the scholar-teacher's individual and collective self interests.

At a practical level, the forces against teaching's being informed by a wider view of scholarship and practiced within a milieu awarding full value for teaching in itself are just as great ... Present American collegiate institutions reflect a century of expanding and building upon an European model that has achieved tremendous success of a kind. Within these structures, a bureaucracy is in place that operates on machine-tooled replaceable parts distributed across the nation. No vice-president or dean is likely to be put in place who does not look remarkably like his predecessor. Chairpersons and division heads reflect the faculties from which they come. Presidents, whose selections are not as tightly controlled by the inner bureaucracy or faculty, still must fit the pattern of trustees overwhelmingly accepting of the university as it is rather than as it might be.

The task ahead is not one of dismantling the pre-eminence of research within American higher education; nor is it to make research a second-class function of the academic community. Further, it is not being suggested that the service function of the academy be demoted to a casual level. Rather, the agenda ahead is to elevate the role of teaching on campus. As suggested by the general public, the question of sound instruction is not an either/or proposition. A high level of instructional effectiveness is an expectation of the professoriate and a requirement for the individuals involved in fulfilling the responsibility. Teaching commands a level of attention commensurate with the amount of time devoted to it.

The decades following Sputnik witnessed a new level of sophistication and maturity in higher education. Demands resulting from increased public accountability, greater openness in governance, and improved measures of instructional effectiveness have ushered in an era of expanded intellectual/instructional integrity. The groundwork has been completed. It is incumbent that administrators seize this opportunity to restore teaching to its rightful role. The challenges are great. Reversing the ever-growing research trends will be more difficult than starting anew. Normal day-to-day demands can drain leaders emotionally and leave little time and energy for new initiatives. The rewards will be few and the process will be slow. The future demands an academic community that is intellectually alive and instructionally competent.

*Teaching commands a level of attention commensurate with the amount of time devoted to it ... The groundwork has been completed. It is incumbent that administrators seize this opportunity to restore teaching to its rightful role.*

Making the profession of teaching the first obligation of the college teacher suggests a totally new orientation for instructional effectiveness. It mandates reform in the way in which professionals are introduced to teaching in their doctoral programs. It escalates the faculty renewal and evaluation trends already under way. It challenges the reward systems that consistently give greater lip service than cash to teaching. It reaffirms the needs of the profession to regulate itself by evaluating classroom and disciplinary competence.

It calls upon the professoriate to pledge allegiance to disciplinary, departmental, and institutional educational goals. Faculties, administrators, and trustees have a collective responsibility that can be fulfilled effectively and imaginatively only if the respective roles of each segment are carefully defined and carried out. Presidents and chief academic officers must lead. Governing boards must oversee the process. Faculty members must face and live with the substantive issues of assessment, evaluation, and reward.

While the change initiative is a shared responsibility, the primary leadership role is thrust upon the nation's chief academic and executive officers. Faculty members need to be reassured by administrators that this is not another log-rolling exercise and that their actions will be supported. Signs of strong leadership must be demonstrated so faculty members will join the movement. Leadership that bonds faculty and administrative efforts into a united front must be forthcoming. Administrators must be willing to take bold stands to support teaching, energetically support new teaching initiatives, and create imaginative ways to enhance the basic instructional function. Administrators must build an attitude and environment that fosters quality teaching. Action needs to be taken that reduces the faculty's fear of evaluation, that eliminates the chronic curricular paralysis present on many campuses, and that balances excessive departmental autonomy with a concern for the total educational process.

---

*Administrators must be willing to take bold stands to support teaching, energetically support new teaching initiatives, and create imaginative ways to enhance the basic instructional function. Administrators must build an attitude and environment that fosters quality teaching.*

---

As with all change initiatives, administrators need to act prudently. They must be willing to assess the current situation, develop plans of action, guide the evolutionary change process, take bold stands when necessary, and build a willingness on campus to adopt those practices that support excellence in the classroom. While each campus will have its own agenda and means to initiate the necessary changes, the guideposts that follow suggest directions for strong administrative leadership. These initiatives can produce a new environment in which teaching and scholarly excellence are the standard for all instructional professionals.

> • **The leadership challenge is to create an environment in which the goals of the institution, interests of the faculty, and needs of the students are balanced.** Departmental and disciplinary activities appropriately command the primary attention of the faculty. While these interests are understandable, what all too often gets lost in the process is the faculty and institutional commitment to students. Institutional goals can shape some of this activity and publicly promote those activities that demonstrate instructional success. Outstanding teaching can be a means of demonstrating the high priority given to meeting the needs of students. While most institutions meet their basic institutional obligations satisfactorily, they are not always effectively fulfilled. Similarly, the educational needs of the students are sometimes displaced by personal and institutional priorities. Since it is the most basic and sometimes referred to as the most routine function, teaching needs continuous attention. By its very nature, specific efforts are needed to keep teaching in the forefront of the academic community.

> • **The leadership challenge is to create an environment in which institutional prestige is demonstrated by how well students are taught and by the quality of research produced.** A casual perusal of promotional materials, recruitment booklets, and institutional summaries quickly reveals that research and scholarly activity are the primary missions of many institutions. A somewhat more thorough review of budgets and how institutional leaders spend their time corroborates this perception. The primary function of all institutions, however, is teaching and it must be so conveyed. Assessment measures need to be developed and used to demonstrate instructional effectiveness. Award and

recognition programs need to be used to focus greater attention on the teaching function. Faculty rewards and administrative time allocations need to reflect the balance needed between the teaching and scholarship functions of the institution.

• **The leadership challenge is to create an environment in which measures of success and accountability are provided throughout all degree programs.** No one measure can be used to demonstrate the overall effectiveness of instruction in a particular classroom or for an entire academic program. Specifically stated goals, objectives, and outcomes measures are needed for courses, minors, majors, and the general education program. Such standards are the pillars of the assessment process and can be used to demonstrate success. Academic leaders in the various departments or disciplines must come to agreement on the course and program expectations. Measures of success need to be put in place. Institutional efforts need to be implemented to ensure that data are collected and handled in a professional and systematic manner.

• **The leadership challenge is to create an environment in which regular review and evaluation of all instruction provided by the institution occurs.** The systematic review of all instruction is a place in which most institutions have significant weaknesses. Most departments, divisions, and institutions are woefully lacking in their ability to evaluate instruction. When attention is given to evaluation, it is commonly limited to full-time (commonly untenured) faculty members. Institutions must demonstrate their concern for the quality of all instruction.Standards and procedures must be implemented for the evaluation of all instructional staff members (full- or part-time and graduate assistants), regardless of faculty rank or tenure status. Similarly, instruction offered at remote sites must stand the same tests of rigor as instruction offered on campus.

• **The leadership challenge is to create an environment in which teaching effectiveness is assessed, evaluated, and improved.** The evaluation of instruction has long been the Achilles' heel of higher education. Many faculty members have a negative attitude toward evaluation. Some faculty members have even mistakenly tried to hide behind the facade of academic freedom. The fear of evaluation must be overcome. Evidence of effective teaching needs to be generated so sophisticated reward systems can be implemented. The time has come for faculty members to develop skills in using evaluative materials to improve instruction and to recognize their obligations to be evaluated on the degree to which they fulfill their professional responsibilities. The internal and external demands for accountability must prevail. Simultaneously, instructional development units should be expanded to respond to the growing needs for faculty renewal.

• **The leadership challenge is to create an environment in which a recognition and reward system that effectively considers the integral nature of scholarship and teaching is supported.** Faculty most often cite the failure of the reward system as the reason for the lack of attention given to teaching. While this may be partially true, substantial changes in the reward structure will not be forthcoming until new evaluative approaches are introduced. Data and information are needed that properly assess classroom preparation, organization, and performance as well as content competence. One's teaching competence and subject matter competence cannot be separated. The profession can no longer tolerate the outstanding classroom performer with little or no scholarship or the great scholar with little or no teaching skill.

• **The leadership challenge is to create an environment in which the multiple functions of teaching, including content, course, curriculum, and instructional development activities, are reviewed.** Most approaches to faculty evaluation place emphasis on the actual functions that occur in the classroom. Much of this evaluation is typically limited to the collection of student input. This process needs to be greatly expanded. As a minimum, periodic peer and department chairperson in-class reviews need to be scheduled throughout one's academic career. The review of teaching also needs to be extended to include course preparation, organization and performance; course and curriculum development; and subject matter competence. The assessment of one's scholarship must be incorporated into the evaluation process of the teaching function. The sole reliance of validating scholarship by outside means (e.g., publications and research grants) must be set aside. Internal validation processes of scholarship must be established.

• **The leadership challenge is to create an environment in which teaching is conceived as an integral component in the doctoral program of all higher education personnel.** The graduate school socialization process has long been identified as an insurmountable impediment to the process of elevating the importance of teaching. For more than a decade, articles and chapters have been written on the need to change doctoral programs, but little movement has resulted. This situation can no longer be accepted. Faculty members must be equipped with teaching and research skills. Significant modifications are required for those interested in entering the higher education profession. Assurances must be made that prospective faculty members understand current learning theory; can demonstrate skill in various modes of instruction; can effectively present lessons and prepare examinations; and can design course materials, select readings and laboratory materials, and evaluate student work. Campus leaders must insist on these knowledges and skills as a minimum.

• **The leadership challenge is to create an environment in which research on teaching in each discipline is stimulated and data to improve instruction are systematically collected.** The teaching aspect of most disciplines is severely neglected. Each discipline serves as a legitimate scholarly area that could be used to effectively blend disciplinary and pedagogical interests. The modification of regular instructional modes to directly involve students in research activities also serves as a means of combining instruction and research. On an institutional level, the assessment of instructional materials along with the regular collection and use of data on instructional effectiveness can be important ingredients in the overall effort to improve instruction. Changes must be made to integrate these efforts into normal promotion, tenure, and self-improvement processes.

• **The leadership challenge is to create an environment in which administrators are encouraged to regularly affirm the importance of teaching and to take actions that demonstrate its significance.** It is critically important that administrators use every possible occasion to reinforce the significance of teaching. Such actions can be demonstrated by specially designed news releases that promote outstanding teaching among the faculty; through specific references to teaching excellence in speeches, memos, and position papers; and the highlighting of outstanding teaching at various recognition ceremonies. Curricular and instructional development activities can be emphasized. The remodeling of a classroom can be effectively used to symbolize the importance of teaching. Teaching deserves special recognition whenever it can be achieved. Of course, formal statements can be made in the application of teaching excellence in promotion, tenure, and other personnel actions.

• **The leadership challenge is to create an environment in which the campus has assessed the status of teaching and has constructed a plan to strengthen its commitment.** Every campus has its own unique character and presents varying opportunities for change. While an increased level of attention placed on teaching will likely draw faculty support, any long-term initiative will require sustained action. Major shifts in attitudes, changes in policies, and modifications in actions do not happen overnight. Likewise, they do not occur without conscious effort. Like any change process, there is a need to assess campus attitudes, review relevant policies, and explore possible alternatives. There is a need to build faculty ownership and to develop administrative support for these efforts. Finally, there is a need to take action in a calculated manner. The plan need not be detailed, but the overall direction of the campus initiatives must be well understood.

## Leadership Opportunity

Naturally, institutions will vary in the degree of commitment that already has been made or needs to be made to the teaching agenda. The choice that remains is not a question of either/or. Rather, the question before each chief academic and executive officer is how far can the institution be moved and what steps can be taken to raise the level of institutional commitment to the primary function of teaching.

While individual responses will vary from one campus to another in form and substance, many of the same basic questions must be raised. The time has come for the academic community to restore teaching to its rightful role. As a beginning, answers are needed for several very basic questions:

- How can the teaching scholar concept be best implemented?

- How can the false dichotomy between teaching and research be set aside so quality instruction can be elevated in its importance?

- What changes can occur in the evaluation of scholarship to lessen the "publish-or-perish" syndrome and improve classroom instruction?

- What changes need to be made in the processes dealing with faculty selection, promotion, tenure, and rewards to better promote effective teaching?

- How can faculty evaluation procedures be improved to promote both self-improvement and performance appraisal?

- How can research on teaching be enhanced to promote more effective instruction?

- What support systems (individual and institutional) are needed to strengthen the teaching/learning process?

- How can institutional leaders better promote, highlight, and encourage instructional development?

The debate must start! The challenge must be met!

## THE BEGINNING

# SELECTED BIBLIOGRAPHY

(1) Baldwin, Roger G. (ed.). **Incentives for Faculty Vitality.** San Francisco: Jossey-Bass Publications, New Directions for Higher Education, 1986.

(2) Carnegie Foundation for the Advancement of Teaching, "The Faculty: Deeply Troubled." **Change** (September/October 1985), pp. 31-34.

(3) Clark, Burton R. **The Academic Life: Small Worlds, Different Worlds.** Princeton, N.J.: The Carnegie Foundation for the Advancement of Teaching, 1987.

(4) Clark, Burton R. "Listening to the Professoriate." **Change** (September/October 1985), pp. 36-43.

(5) Cross, Patricia K. "In Search of Zippers." **AAHE Bulletin** (June 1988), pp. 3-7.

(6) Boyer, Ernest L. **College: The Undergraduate Experience in America.** New York: Harper & Row Publishers, 1987.

(7) Eble, Kenneth E. **The Aims of College Teaching.** San Francisco: Jossey-Bass Publishers, 1983.

(8) Eble, Kenneth E. **The Craft of Teaching.** San Francisco: Jossey-Bass Publishers, 1977.

(9) Eison, Jim. **Creating Teaching Excellence Programs.** Cape Girardeau, MO: Southeast Missouri State University, Center for Teaching and Learning, 1988.

(10) Fenton, Edwin. **Developing a Culture of Teaching in a Small Research University.** Pittsburgh: Carnegie Mellon University, The University Teaching Center, 1988.

(11) Green, Patricia J., and Stark, Joan. **Approaches to Research on the Improvement of Postsecondary Teaching and Learning.** Ann Arbor, MI: National Center for Research to Improve Postsecondary Teaching and Learning, 1986.

(12) Gaff, Jerry G. **Toward Faculty Renewal.** San Francisco: Jossey-Bass Publishers, 1976.

(13) **Guide to Institutional Planning.** Cape Girardeau, MO: Southeast Missouri State University, Office of the Provost, 1988.

(14) Guskin, Alan E. (ed.). **The Administrator's Role in Effective Teaching**. San Francisco: Jossey-Bass Publishers, New Directions for Teaching and Learning Series, 1981.

(15) Halpen, D.F. (ed.). **Student Outcomes Assessment: What Institutions Stand to Gain.** San Francisco: Jossey-Bass Publishers, New Directions in Higher Education, 1987.

(16) **Integrity in the College Curriculum: A Report to the Academic Community.** Washington, D.C.: Association of American Colleges, 1985.

(17) Katz, Joseph and Henry, Mildred. **Turning Professors into Teachers.** New York: Macmillan Publishing Company, 1988.

(18) Keller, George. **Academic Strategy: The Management Revolution in American Higher Education.** Baltimore: The Johns Hopkins University Press, 1983.

(19) "The Letter: 37 Presidents Write." **AAHE Bulletin** (November 1987), pp. 10-13.

(20) Lee, Calvin B.T. (ed.). **Improving College Teaching.** Washington, D.C.: American Council on Education, 1967.

(21)   Marincovich, Michele. (ed.). **Teaching at Stanford: An Introductory Handbook for Faculty, Academic Staff/Teaching, and Teaching Assis tants.** Stanford, CA: Stanford University, The Center for Teaching and Learning, 1987.

(22)   Mayhew, Lewis B., and Ford, Patrick J. **Reform in Graduate and Professional Education.** San Francisco: Jossey-Bass Publishers, 1974.

(23)   **A New Vitality in General Education.** Washington, D.C.: Association of American Colleges, 1988.

(24)   Peterson, Marvin W., Cameron, Kim S., Mets, Lisa A., Jones, Philip, and Ethington, Deborah. **The Organizational Context for Teaching and Learning.** Ann Arbor, MI: National Center for Research to Improve Postsecondary Teaching and Learning, 1986.

(25)   **To Secure the Blessings of Liberty.** Washington, D.C.: Association of American Colleges, 1986.

(26)   Sheridan, Harriet W. "The Compleat Professor, Jr." **AAHE Bulletin** (December, 1988), pp. 3-7.

(27)   Southerland, Arthur R., and Butera, Roberta Jacobs. "Barriers to Teaching." **American School and University** (August 1986), pp. 32d+.

(28)   **University of Idaho Long-Range Plan.** Moscow, ID: University of Idaho, Office of the Academic Vice President, 1984.

(29)   Wagner, Jon. "Teaching and Research as Student Responsibilities." **Change** (September/October 1987). pp. 26-35.

(30)   Wodsworth, Emily C. (ed.). **A Handbook for New Practitioners.** Stillwater, OK: New Forums Press, The Professional and Organizational Development Network in Higher Education, 1988.

# APPENDIX A

## A National Survey of Chief Academic Officers on the Level of Commitment to Instructional Effectiveness

**Purpose:** This study is designed to assess the perceptions and attitudes of chief academic officers regarding the level of institutional commitment to instructional effectiveness. The survey is being sent to academic officers in four-year colleges and universities across the nation. The primary goal of the study is to collect information on specific and general areas affecting instruction on campus. The focus of the study is on specific factors external to the classroom that impact and shape instructional experiences.

**Commitment should be judged in terms of the amount of time, energy, and resources your institution devotes to the particular function. A high level of commitment indicates that there are visible examples of substantial investment in the specific area. A low level of commitment implies that little effort has been made in the area (very little discussion, no policies, no expenditure of time or resources).**

**Directions:** Please respond to each item by circling the number from 1 (low) to 10 (high) that best represents your institution's commitment to an area. If a specific activity does not occur on your campus, please circle 0. Leave blank any item you feel unable to evaluate.

| | Level of Commitment | | | |
|---|---|---|---|---|
| **Instructional Development Activities** | **None** | **Low** | **(circle)** | **High** |

1. Workshops/seminars on effective instruction are conducted for new full-time faculty members.

   0  1  2  3  4  5  6  7  8  9  10

2. Seminars/workshops on teaching are held for graduate teaching assistants.

   0  1  2  3  4  5  6  7  8  9  10

3. Faculty seminars, workshops, and conferences on teaching and learning are conducted on campus.

   0  1  2  3  4  5  6  7  8  9  10

4. The campus maintains various colleague support mechanisms (mentors, chairperson monitoring, etc.) to promote and support effective instruction.

   0  1  2  3  4  5  6  7  8  9  10

5. Effective instruction is promoted by an organized unit or program (e.g., center for teaching and learning).

   0  1  2  3  4  5  6  7  8  9  10

| | Level of Commitment | | | |
|---|---|---|---|---|
| **Instructional Enhancement Efforts** | **None** | **Low** | **(circle)** | **High** |

6. Librarians are used to promote effective instruction on campus.

   0  1  2  3  4  5  6  7  8  9  10

7. Released time and financial awards are used to promote teaching improvement.

   0  1  2  3  4  5  6  7  8  9  10

8. Funds are available to support instructional improvement items (e.g., conferences on instructional effectiveness, faculty development activities, and other instructional improvement items.)

   0  1  2  3  4  5  6  7  8  9  10

9. Curriculum development activities are given high visibility to illustrate their importance.

   0  1  2  3  4  5  6  7  8  9  10

10. Administrators regularly emphasize the ways research and scholarly activity can be used to reinforce or support effective teaching.

    0  1  2  3  4  5  6  7  8  9  10

| | Level of Commitment | | | |
|---|---|---|---|---|
| **Employment Policies and Practices** | **None** | **Low** | **(circle)** | **High** |

11. A faculty member's teaching effectiveness is evaluated as a significant/integral aspect of the initial hiring process.

0 1 2 3 4 5 6 7 8 9 10

12. Classroom instruction is regularly evaluated by students.

0 1 2 3 4 5 6 7 8 9 10

13. Teaching effectiveness is evaluated as a significant/integral aspect of the tenure process.

0 1 2 3 4 5 6 7 8 9 10

14. Teaching effectiveness is evaluated as a significant/integral aspect of the promotion process.

0 1 2 3 4 5 6 7 8 9 10

15. Teaching recognition programs (grants, awards, etc.) that promote effective teaching are available.

0 1 2 3 4 5 6 7 8 9 10

| | Level of Commitment | | | |
|---|---|---|---|---|
| **Strategic Administrative Actions** | **None** | **Low** | **(circle)** | **High** |

16. The importance of teaching is emphasized by upper level administrators in speeches and public presentations.

0 1 2 3 4 5 6 7 8 9 10

17. News releases and articles are regularly used to focus attention on exciting classroom activities.

0 1 2 3 4 5 6 7 8 9 10

18. Research designed to improve the quality of instruction is regularly conducted on campus.

0 1 2 3 4 5 6 7 8 9 10

19. Institutional data on teaching effectiveness are collected and used as a means to improve instruction on campus.

0 1 2 3 4 5 6 7 8 9 10

20. Academic administrators across campus regularly reinforce the importance of effective teaching.

0 1 2 3 4 5 6 7 8 9 10

| | Level of Commitment | | | |
|---|---|---|---|---|
| **Campus Environment and Culture** | **None** | **Low** | **(circle)** | **High** |

1. Faculty have a clear sense of ownership of the curriculum and other instructional concerns.  
0 1 2 3 4 5 6 7 8 9 10

2. The level of intellectual vitality and morale on campus is conducive to effective instruction.  
0 1 2 3 4 5 6 7 8 9 10

23. The faculty have a clear sense of confidence in the upper administrative leadership that fosters effective instruction.  
0 1 2 3 4 5 6 7 8 9 10

24. There is a clear sense of administrative stability that allows faculty to focus on the instructional process.  
0 1 2 3 4 5 6 7 8 9 10

25. There is a shared feeling of institutional pride that stimulates effective classroom performance.  
0 1 2 3 4 5 6 7 8 9 10

Using the previous statements asoperational definitions of the category listed below, rate your satisfaction with the level of **Institutional Performance** in each area.

| | Level of Satisfaction | | | |
|---|---|---|---|---|
| | **None** | **Low** | **(circle)** | **High** |
| Instructional Development Activities | 0 1 2 | 3 4 5 | 6 7 8 | 9 10 |
| Instructional Enhancement Efforts | 0 1 2 | 3 4 5 | 6 7 8 | 9 10 |
| Employment Policies and Practices | 0 1 2 | 3 4 5 | 6 7 8 | 9 10 |
| Strategic Administrative Actions | 0 1 2 | 3 4 5 | 6 7 8 | 9 10 |
| Campus Environment and Culture | 0 1 2 | 3 4 5 | 6 7 8 | 9 10 |

Please rate your satisfaction with the amount of **Personal Attention** you devote to each area.

| | Level of Satisfaction | | | |
|---|---|---|---|---|
| | **None** | **Low** | **(circle)** | **High** |
| Instructional Development Activities | 0 1 2 | 3 4 5 | 6 7 8 | 9 10 |
| Instructional Enhancement Efforts | 0 1 2 | 3 4 5 | 6 7 8 | 9 10 |
| Employment Policies and Practices | 0 1 2 | 3 4 5 | 6 7 8 | 9 10 |
| Strategic Administrative Actions | 0 1 2 | 3 4 5 | 6 7 8 | 9 10 |
| Campus Environment and Culture | 0 1 2 | 3 4 5 | 6 7 8 | 9 10 |